Mentoring
BEGINNING
TEACHERS

Second Edition

Mentoring
BEGINNING
TEACHERS

Guiding, Reflecting, Coaching

Stenhouse Publishers
Portland, Maine

Jean
BOREEN

Mary K.
JOHNSON

Donna
NIDAY

Joe
POTTS

Stenhouse Publishers
www.stenhouse.com

Credits
Cover photograph of Jeanie McElvain and Cassie Bliek, Boone Middle School, Boone, Iowa, by Don Payne, Iowa State University.

Library of Congress Cataloging-in-Publication Data
Mentoring beginning teachers : guiding, reflecting, coaching / Jean Boreen ... [et al.]. -- 2nd ed.
    p. cm.
Includes bibliographical references.
ISBN 978-1-57110-742-8 (alk. paper)
1. Mentoring in education--United States. 2. First year teachers--United States. I. Boreen, Jean.
LB1731.4.M4655 2009
371.102--dc22

2008035175

Cover, interior design, and typesetting by Designboy Creative Group.
Manufactured in the United States of America on acid-free, recycled paper.
15 14 13 12 11 10 09 9 8 7 6 5 4 3 2 1

We dedicate this book to
our new colleagues in the teaching profession
and the mentors they will become.

CONTENTS

11

12

13

PREFACE

When we cast our bread upon the waters we can presume
that someone downstream whose face we may never see
will benefit from our action, even as we enjoy the gifts
sent to us from a donor upstream.

—Maya Angelou

This book has grown out of our own mentoring experiences and studies and from a philosophy that advocates listening, questioning, and collaborating. Using these strategies, mentors help beginning teachers to recognize problems and then to find ways of reflecting, talking, and responding. As Maya Angelou states, we may influence many people we never see; mentors influence beginning teachers' current and future students, making the role of mentoring a vital one for the education profession.

We appreciated the warm responses we received to our first book, as well as the questions and suggestions from mentors at workshops and conferences in the United States and Canada. We have integrated this information into this new edition and have updated all of the chapters.

We have added 40 percent new material to this second edition, including chapters on mentoring the beginning teacher in negotiating the school culture, collaborating with parents, teaching English language learners, preparing for curriculum mapping, and working with administrators. We have also retained the individual mentoring approach while adding team mentoring strategies. We hope that this second edition will provide an even greater service as a practical and theoretical guide for mentors to start beginning teachers on successful paths toward student learning and teacher professional development.

In conveying our philosophy, we use a number of terms in particular ways: the phrase *beginning teachers* includes student teachers as well as teachers in their first, second, or possibly third year of teaching; *mentor* refers to an experienced teacher who works with colleagues new to the profession; and *mentoring* represents the approach of guiding, reflecting, and coaching.

Although we discuss the major concerns and successes of the beginning teaching experience, we realize that mentoring relationships are not universal and that this book cannot cover all areas of classroom practice. We hope that it will nevertheless be helpful to K–12 mentors, administrators establishing a mentoring program, university teacher educators working with mentors and beginning teachers, and beginning teachers themselves.

Each chapter presents a key question. We begin by asking, "Why Do I Want to Be Part of a Mentoring Experience?" and consider why mentors find professional and personal satisfaction in assisting the progress of beginning teachers. Chapter 2 asks, "Why Do We Need Mentors?" and offers a brief history of mentoring that establishes the need for mentors in the schools and examines the benefits and tensions that often accompany the mentoring relationship. This chapter also includes recommendations for successful mentoring.

Chapters 3, 4, and 5 provide specific mentoring strategies. Chapter 3 asks, "How Do I Prepare to Be a Mentoring Guide?" and includes specific suggestions to use before and after the arrival of the beginning teacher. Chapter 4 asks, "How Do I Prepare to Be a Mentoring Coach?" and discusses ways to use questioning and mirroring techniques to model decision-making strategies for preplanning and postreflection. This chapter also provides examples of numerous ways to help beginning teachers understand what is happening in the classroom. Chapter 5 asks, "How Do I Encourage Reflection?" and considers strategies that stimulate reflection and dialogue between mentors and beginning teachers. This chapter also presents a rationale for the practice of reflection.

Chapters 6 and 7 focus on specific classroom situations and learners. Chapter 6 asks, "How Do I Help with Classroom Management Challenges?" and delineates useful suggestions for that most difficult challenge: managing the classroom for optimal student success. Chapter 7 asks, "How Do I Encourage Teachers Who Work with English Language Learners?" and describes ways to assist beginning teachers in their work with English language learners and collaborations with ELL teachers.

Chapters 8, 9, 10, and 11 look at the school system itself, including school culture, parents, curriculum, and administrators. Chapter 8 asks, "How Do I Help Integrate Beginning Teachers into the School Culture?" and provides suggestions for viewing the school culture from an outsider's perspective as well as helping new teachers become an integral part of the faculty. Chapter 9 asks, "How Do I Promote Effective Relationships with Parents/Guardians?" and describes ways mentors can help beginning teachers achieve a positive relationship with parents and guardians. Chapter 10 asks, "How Do I Provide Mentoring Opportunities During Curriculum Mapping?" and focuses on helping beginning teachers obtain a vision for both horizontal and vertical curriculum mapping. Chapter 11 asks, "How Should Mentors Communicate with Administrators?" and describes ways school administrators can work alongside mentors to support the beginning teacher in curricular development, teaching strategies, and professional development.

Next, we move the focus to a long-range perspective of the beginning teacher's professional development. Chapter 12 asks, "How Do I Encourage Professional Development?" and examines ways mentors can help beginning teachers formulate an Individual Professional Development Plan (IPDP) that includes goals, pathways for professional growth, and a portfolio.

The book concludes with helpful mentoring information. Chapter 13, "'What If?' Questions from Mentors," a question-and-answer chapter, looks at theoretical and practical mentoring concerns. A final section entitled "Resources for Teachers" lists books on professional growth for beginning and mentor teachers as well as useful websites that contain further information.

ACKNOWLEDGMENTS

We would like to thank the following people for reading the manuscript and offering suggestions: Pia Alexander, Sandra Bolton, Mark and Sarah Campbell, Marjorie Cleveringa, Kate Gillon, Laura Gray-Rosendale, Sibylle Gruber, Karen Greenstreet, Ronaldo Hartley, Don Hohl, Elizabeth Johnson, Cynthia Kosso, Barb LeClaire, Sandy Moore, M'Liss Patterson, Liisa Potts, Randi Reppen, Sue Slick, Shannon Stanton, Julie and Mike Switzer, and Anne Weir.

We also express appreciation to the Stenhouse editorial staff, and especially to Bill Varner, Chris Downey, and others for their work in helping us shape the manuscript.

We would like to recognize the mentors in our own lives: Leona Bell, Suzanne Bratcher, James Brimeyer, Tony Burgess, Anne DiPardo, Dixie Goswami, Bill Grabe, Haraldine Harbert, Betty Houser, James Marshall, Jane Neff, Jon Schneckloth, Lynn Sorum, Maurice Stamps, Bonnie Sunstein, Bob Tremmel, and Richard Zbaracki.

In addition, we thank the numerous mentors in the public schools with whom we have worked over the years. Their example has helped us formulate the philosophical stance we propose in this book.

Our family and friends have also contributed to this text: Liisa, Julien, and Maxwell Potts; John, Amanda, and Laura Boreen; Ruth Ann Van Donslear; Jeff, Liz, Andrew, Matt, and Joe Johnson; Leila Niday; and Nancy, Ronnie, Jason, Emilie, and Chris Roberts.

1

Why Do I

WANT TO BE PART OF A MENTORING EXPERIENCE?

A success story:

> The last bell for the year rang, and Melanie Spears, a first-year teacher, walked into Anne Davies's classroom. Anne could see the relief and pride on Melanie's face: she had not only survived her first year, she had enjoyed it... mostly. "Thanks so much for your help this year; I couldn't have made it some of those days without your support and great ideas."
>
> Anne replied, "Well, it was fun for me to get to work with you like this. Gets me excited about teaching all over again."
>
> "I'm glad that I was able to give you a little something back for all you gave me. And I already feel good about next year, especially since I know that you'll still be right down the hall."

Something else again...

> Kevin Parker sat in the office of his university supervisor, Carol Mackie, and recounted for her the latest confrontation he had had with his cooperating teacher, Marcus Fry. "Nothing I do is ever good enough for him. I worked and worked on

1

my lesson plan for today, and when I got to school this morning, he looked at it for about three seconds and told me it wouldn't work. When I asked him why, he kind of sneered at me and said if I couldn't figure it out, I probably didn't belong in teaching. Maybe he's right; I just don't have any confidence anymore. He's never told me one thing I've done well, and a couple of times he actually took the class away from me when I was teaching. I guess he wanted to make sure I didn't leave something out, but couldn't he have just told me after class? I could have covered it the next day. I feel about six inches high when he does that. I'll never get those kids to take me seriously now."

When Carol talked to Marcus Fry later that day, she sensed his surprise that Kevin had shared his concerns with her. "Listen, I'm sorry if he's getting touchy about this, but I'm trying to make him into a real teacher. I don't think he's look-ing enough at where this unit needs to go; he only gives me one lesson at a time, and usually it's the morning before he's got to teach it. My kids have tests to take later this year, and I can't afford to have them lose days while Kevin tries to figure out what he wants to accomplish. I keep giving him specific suggestions, and half the time, he doesn't even use them. I didn't want to bring you in before, because I wanted Kevin to try to get a grip on this himself, but if he's just going to come whining to you, then maybe you need to come in here and clarify things for both of us. I'm pretty frustrated with this myself; I've never had a student teacher like this one."

These experiences are dramatic examples of the positive and the negative interactions that can characterize mentoring relationships. Most of us remember how important the student teaching experience was in our professional development; mentoring beginning teachers has become similarly important. In this book, we would like to urge you to consider becoming a mentor teacher and to show you how to take on this role in a most meaningful manner for you and for the new teacher with whom you will work.

Student teaching provides the practical experience students need and want after their long immersion in books, journal articles, and professional and academic conversations. Mentoring helps new teachers in their transition from student to professional. But what will the mentoring experience offer you?

Becoming a mentor—either individually or as a team mentor—allows us to repay the debt we owe to our own mentors, or, if our early years of teaching were painful, to spare other new teachers the same fate. Either way, we offer an invaluable service to our profession. Similarly, serving as a mentor assures us of a lasting impact on how future teachers perform in our chosen field. Because of our own substantial experience, we develop strong feelings about many curricular, student, and professional issues. As mentors we can persuade new members of the profession to bring pedagogical beliefs and techniques we feel are vital into their future classrooms.

Participating in the mentoring experience highlights our professionalism to several important audiences: to our local, regional, and national colleagues; to administrators; to parents; and even to students. We do not often have the opportunity to publicly affirm our status as teachers who excel. Responsibility for mentoring a beginning teacher attests to our achievements in the field and to the confidence of those outside the school in entrusting a young teacher to our care.

Other benefits? Many of us have experienced the isolation of classroom teaching. As Daniel Lortie (1975) notes in *Schoolteacher: A Sociological Study*, one of the most common complaints of teachers is the lack of time for any meaningful collaboration with fellow teachers. We may call to each other across the hall between classes or sit side by side at a faculty meeting, but these instances can hardly provide either personal or professional fulfillment. A beginning teacher with a passionate interest in students and the life of the school can help to meet that need. Furthermore, when the relationship between a mentor and a beginning teacher achieves mutual respect and trust, both may wish to continue their dialogue beyond the official schedule. Mentors often report that this continued contact provides some of their richest collegial interactions.

For those mentoring student teachers, the presence of another professional in the classroom may also provide learning opportunities that their own school's inservices cannot provide. The student teaching semester will undoubtedly connect the mentor teacher to new ideas in the field through conversations with her student teacher and the university supervisor. Interactions with the supervisor may in turn establish stronger university connections for the mentor that can result in opportunities for further collaboration in the classroom and in the university setting. For example, the mentor teacher's classroom might be chosen as a site for university research because of the university supervisor's respect for the mentor teacher's classroom practices.

The potential for classroom-based teacher research represents an additional reason for taking on a student teacher or acting in a mentor role: the extra pair of hands may free the mentor teacher to participate in a university-sponsored research project, or the mentor may be able to devise a project that will gather significant information on the abilities and needs of students and how they are being met in her classroom. Partners in the mentoring relationship also have the option of classroom research, and this, too, can be a source of recognition for the mentor teacher that enhances professional growth.

Leslie Huling lists other benefits, including increased professionalism, reflection, renewal and reenergizing, professional satisfaction, and leadership opportunities. She states, "Because mentors can exert substantially greater influence on the school organization than novices, the benefits mentors derive from mentoring may be of equal, or even greater, importance than those experienced by novice teachers" (2001, 3).

The mentoring experience is undoubtedly a challenge. As a mentor, you will be asked to play the dual roles of host and colleague. If you are working with a student teacher, you will also need to balance "parenting" your charge with being a "sibling" to the university supervisor as the two of you negotiate how best to work with the student. And all of this will take place in conjunction with the responsibilities you already have to the students in your class. In our view, the potential advantages to inviting a student teacher into your classroom or mentoring a new colleague far outweigh the disadvantages. We hope this book will help to make the mentoring experience a fulfilling one for all concerned.

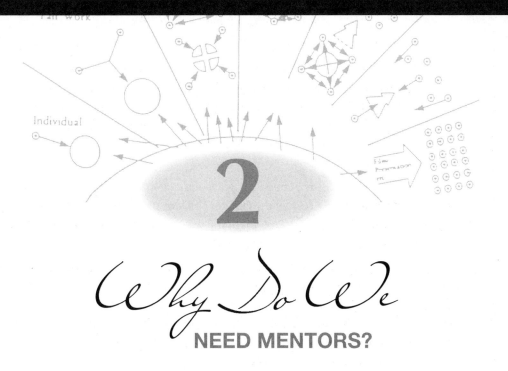

2

Why Do We
NEED MENTORS?

Is it realistic to expect teachers to teach enthusiastically hour after hour, day after day, sensitively diagnosing and remedying learning difficulties? During each of these hours . . . teachers make 200 or more decisions.

—John Goodlad, *A Place Called School*

How can mentors help beginning teachers become effective decision makers in the classroom? How can they help them develop their strengths and negotiate differences? Which factors enhance collaborative relationships and which discourage them? In this chapter we discuss the need for mentoring and its benefits as well as the accompanying tensions.

✍ · The Need for Mentoring · ✍

Eileen and Wayne, both veteran teachers, listened as the professional development leader told them, "Turn to a partner and talk about the time when you were a beginning teacher and about the people who mentored you." The assignment came in the midst of a three-day inservice for beginning teachers and mentors.

The workshop had started with general introductions and then a scavenger hunt in which mentoring pairs had searched for clues in various parts of the building, a strategy aimed at helping beginning teachers feel more at ease in their new environment. Now the beginning teachers were meeting together in one room to share their concerns, and the mentors in another to discuss their own experiences when they entered the profession.

"Well," said Wayne, as he rubbed his gray mustache, "I don't think I had any mentors. I had some pretty bad times, though. The kids pretty much got the best of me that first year." He chuckled, "My planning was rotten, too. Sometimes I didn't know what I was going to teach the next day or even the next period."

"That sounds pretty familiar," said Eileen. "I remember one time during my first year when two teachers asked me if we could put three sections of seventh graders together to watch a film. Once the film started, the two teachers said they had to go prepare for their after-school coaching assignments. They left me alone on a Friday afternoon with seventy-five seventh graders." She threw up her arms and exclaimed, "As you can guess, it was chaos!"

Wayne laughed. "It sounds as if you had tormentors instead of mentors."

Eileen nodded. "It's a wonder that I didn't quit after that first year."

"Uh-huh. At first, when the principal asked me to be a mentor this year, I just thought it was mollycoddling these young kids. But after I heard the statistics about the numbers who leave teaching, I changed my mind. Being a mentor is a pretty important job."

The low numbers of beginning teachers who remain in the profession do seem daunting. Despite their initial enthusiasm, far too many abandon the profession, depressed and discouraged. The National Commission on Teaching and America's Future (2003) reported the following national attrition data: 14 percent of beginning teachers leave after the first year; 24 percent after two years; 33 percent after three years; 40 percent after four years; and 46 percent after five years. In fact, the National Center for Education Statistics reports that "the attrition rates of new teachers are five times higher than those of their more experienced counterparts" (1999, 5). A prior study by Frank Gonzales and Alicia Sosa (1993) indicated that the most talented beginning teachers are sometimes those most apt to leave. This has led Joan Montgomery Halford to refer to education as "the profession which eats its young" (1998, 33). The National Commission on Teaching and America's Future estimates that teacher turnover costs the nation's school districts approximately $7 billion annually for recruiting, hiring, and training (Dillon 2007). To ensure that future students will be challenged to think and learn, it is imperative that the educational community find a way to retain the talented teachers who are leaving the profession.

In *Schoolteacher: A Sociological Study*, Dan Lortie identifies isolation as a major cause of new teacher attrition: teachers are compartmentalized into "egg-crate classrooms." The "cellular nature of schools" fosters independence and self-reliance but discourages collaboration (1975, 14). While many elementary and middle school teachers may be involved in grade-level or interdisciplinary teams, high school teachers enjoy fewer opportunities for collaboration. As Simon, a beginning high school teacher, remarked, "As a first-year teacher, I missed the collaborative spirit of sharing unit plan ideas with my college student peers. Class preparation seems to be more work than enjoyment."

Peggy Ishler lists other problems for the beginning teacher, including, "too high [self] expectations . . . , lack of encouragement or help from fellow teachers, and a principal who may give frequent criticism and no support" (1998, 9a). These factors, along with low salaries, have caused many beginning teachers, including Ishler's own daughter-in-law Kathie, to seek other careers.

The need to retain beginning teachers is compounded by job market prospects. Because of the baby boomer retirements, the New York City school system, the nation's largest, hired approximately 6,300 new teachers in 2007. California projects that it will need one hundred thousand new teachers over the next decade (Dillon 2007). Thomas G. Carroll, president of the National Commission on Teaching and America's Future, estimates that more than one million teachers (one-third of the nation's teachers) are baby boomers but explains, "The real school staffing issue is teacher retention, not recruitment. America produces enough teachers each year to fill the schools, but it loses them like water draining through a leaky bucket. They leave for many reasons, but lack of support is at the top of the list" (2005, 199). Mentoring thus becomes even more vital.

In 2004, thirty-three states reported that they required mandated mentoring programs, but only twenty-two states said they required and financed mentoring for all beginning teachers (Hall 2005), even though research indicates that mentoring can significantly reduce attrition. Sandra Odell (1992) found that the attrition rate for teachers receiving one year of mentoring was only 16 percent after four years of teaching, about half the national attrition rate at that time. These factors caused the National Center for Education Statistics to conclude in its report that "mentoring relationships play a critical role in the support, training, and retention of new teachers" (1999, 5).

The workshop director asked individuals to share their experiences. Eileen and Wayne listened as Meridee, now in her seventh year of teaching kindergarten, gave a personal testimony: "The first years are all about survival. If I hadn't had

Theresa as my mentor, I would have been out of here after the first year—maybe even the first semester. I would have missed out on the excitement I feel each year when I see a new set of learners enter my door."

Recalling their own experiences with students over the years, Eileen and Wayne nodded, and Wayne remarked, "I'm starting to be convinced that this mentoring thing is pretty important in keeping good teachers."

"You're right. It's kind of like a legacy. It reminds me of when my own children started riding bikes." When Wayne frowned in confusion, Eileen explained, "I didn't just send them out the door. I first showed them how to ride a tricycle, then a bike with trainer wheels, and then the real bike. I stood beside them until they could pedal down the sidewalk by themselves." She paused and then added, "And then I had a box of Band-Aids handy, ready for their falls."

Wayne laughed. "Well, I'm convinced that we have a mighty important role as mentors, but I'm not so convinced that this next part of the agenda is important. It says that one teacher will narrate and others will mime the history of mentoring. Now why do we have to know the history?"

Eileen smirked, "You're a social studies teacher, and you don't know the importance of history! Don't you tell your students that it's important to learn about the past?"

"OK, OK, you win."

✒ · An Overview of Mentoring · ✒

As Wayne and Eileen learned, mentoring has a long history, possibly dating as far back as the eighteenth century B.C., when the laws of Hammurabi of Babylon required artisans to teach their craft to younger students. The practice of apprenticeship continued through the centuries and was modified at the beginning of the twentieth century, when business and industry adopted the apprenticeship model. James Cash (J. C.) Penney is credited as the father of business mentoring. He required each of his store managers to train a newcomer, who then founded another Penney's store.

Education, for good or ill, has adopted many of the practices of the business world, including mentoring. In England, starting with the Industrial Revolution, teachers served apprenticeships as "pupil teachers." This educational concept was introduced in the United States in the mid-1800s, when apprenticed teachers, who took no education courses, were expected to follow in the footsteps of an experienced teacher, replicating the "expert's" teaching style and methods. In the 1920s, states began requiring education courses. By the 1950s, many teacher education institutions had changed the term "practice teaching" to "student teaching" and the term "teacher training" to "teacher education" (Furlong and Maynard 1995), changes in practice and wording that reflected shifts in thinking about the practice of neophyte teachers. In the 1980s, various commissions urged the mentoring of beginning teachers (Carnegie 1986, Holmes 1986, National Commission on Excellence in Education 1983). This caused many states to mandate mentoring programs, and Leslie Huling-Austin referred to teacher induction as "sweeping the entire nation, making it one of the fastest growing educational movements in recent history" (1990, 538).

Today we recognize that students and new teachers, as adult learners, have different learning styles as well as "multiple intelligences" (Gardner 2006). We have moved away from thinking that beginning teachers should mimic or copy the methods of experienced teachers. The emphasis now is on new teachers becoming reflective thinkers who explore their own individual teaching styles. Teacher education institutes also have begun to recognize the need for classroom experience early in teacher education preparation, and many have formed partnerships with elementary and secondary schools to establish professional development programs for beginning teachers (Darling-Hammond 2005, Teitel 2003).

Over time our teaching philosophy has changed from one that is teacher dominated to one that is student centered. Similarly, we have witnessed a change in the preparation of preservice teachers. The "pupil teacher" in the eighteenth century shadowed a master teacher and copied his techniques, thereby gaining practice without theory. In later times, colleges supplied theory and the student teaching experience provided practice, but a sharp division existed between the two stages.

In the past, the novice teacher worked with an experienced teacher only during the student-teaching stage. Today, however, most teacher education institutes link theory and practice, working closely with schools early in a preservice teacher's career and sometimes through the third year of teaching. In this way, students can relate the "what"—the practice of teaching—to the "why"—the theories underlying the practice—to better understand why a particular practice does or does not work in the classroom.

Many universities have adopted the term *mentor* in place of *cooperating teacher*. A mentor is a veteran teacher who works with a novice during the beginning teacher's early experiences in the classroom. In the past, a novice merely watched and observed. Today, however, a beginning teacher is encouraged to be an active participant, inquirer, and critical thinker. The mentor's role has also changed, from that of advice-giver and problem-solver to questioner, listener, and model for reflective thinking (Furlong and Maynard 1995).

As the narrator concluded the skit, Eileen and Wayne once again shared their reactions.

"I had a practicum student last year who was in her sophomore year at college," Eileen said. "I like the fact that more universities and colleges are placing their teacher education students in the schools earlier and for more semesters."

"Me, too," Wayne rejoined. "I had a student teacher last spring, and he was a whole lot more comfortable because of all his experience during other semesters. That was sure different from my own experience. I remember that I was shaking from head to foot."

"Did you hear that they're now calling us mentors when we have student teachers in the room?" Eileen asked. "I guess I didn't really think of myself as a mentor, but I was."

"Me, too. I felt like I didn't know what I was doing, though, in working with my student teacher—just as I don't really know what I can do to help Karla during her first year."

"I guess that's why we're here. What's next on the agenda?"

"It says 'Mentoring Benefits.' Chuck told me that he was going to do that part. He's going to explain a study that showed what first-year teachers said were the best kinds of mentoring help."

"Sounds good."

⤞ · Mentoring Benefits · ⤞

In addition to encouraging beginning teachers to remain in the teaching profession, effective mentoring assists them in numerous other ways. Surveys of beginning teachers have found that they rank emotional support, which reduces their sense of isolation, as the most helpful factor in their development (Odell 1992). Studies of new teachers in the Santa Cruz New Teacher Project indicate increased job satisfaction, higher retention, greater effectiveness with diverse students, and better instructional problem solving as a result of being mentored. Furthermore, the principals cited "better new-teacher morale, increased willingness to take risks, more effective problem solving strategies, improved classroom management and organization, and more effective instructional strategies" (Moir, Gless, and Baron 1999). The word *support* appears many times in the beginning teacher studies, indicating how important it is for beginning teachers that others in the profession are willing to help make their first years of teaching effective, productive experiences.

When a new teacher becomes more effective in the classroom, the potential for student learning increases. Research indicates that mentoring new teachers can increase their students' motivation and critical thinking skills (Summers 1987). Thus, mentors can be sure that they play an important role in assisting a beginning teacher not only to develop competence but also to remain in the profession longer.

"Support, huh?" Wayne murmured. "Well, I know all about support—I have two kids in college. They call all the time asking for support."

Eileen smiled. "Now, Wayne, I bet you give them more than just a few dollars. I bet you give them emotional support, too."

"I guess so. Emotional, instructional, and classroom management support—I guess I can handle that. What is next on the agenda?"

"Next are the mentoring recommendations."

"Good," said Wayne. "Now we're getting to what I really need to hear."

✍ · Mentoring Recommendations · ✍

A number of factors can aid or hinder the mentoring relationship. It may be helpful to be aware of these factors in order to build on the strengths of the situation and find ways to counter potential problems. An effective mentor listens, communicates, understands students, knows the content area, and is willing to aid the growth of a beginning teacher (Brock and Grady 1997). For first-year teachers, choosing one's own mentor is considered the most valid way to achieve high mutual regard (Odell 1990). However, it might require delaying mentor pairing until partway through the school year when the beginning teacher has become well enough acquainted with colleagues to select a mentor. Most school systems with a mentoring program provide assigned mentors who are usually designated by an administrator.

The following factors should be considered in forming a mentoring partnership. If possible, a mentor should

- Have a minimum of three to five years of teaching experience.

- Be teaching in the same content area or at the same grade level as the beginning teacher.

- Have a classroom close to that of the beginning teacher.

- Be significantly older than the beginning teacher.

- Be aware of gender differences, although the importance of this factor may depend upon circumstances.

A mentor should have at least three to five years of teaching experience so that he or she is viewed as a veteran teacher rather than as a peer (Slick 1995). Beginning teachers, even highly competent beginning teachers, need time for their own development. They should not be spending time as an official mentor.

If the mentor and the beginning teacher share the same content area or the same or similar grade level, the mentor is usually able to provide more direct assistance. This commonsense factor suggests that a first-grade teacher may be of more help to a beginning first-grade teacher than a sixth-grade teacher would, or that a math teacher might assist another math teacher better than a vocal music teacher could.

However, in grade levels or departments with mostly new teachers or in small school districts or small school buildings, mentors may need to cross grade levels or curriculum boundaries. The mentoring relationship can still be highly productive if the mentor is a skilled professional and if the beginning teacher feels confident in the area of content knowledge. In one secondary school, for example, Ben, an art teacher, mentored Jason, a beginning social studies teacher, with surprisingly effective results. The art teacher provided the social studies teacher with useful ideas; for example, having the students work in groups to create cartoons or murals of various time periods. The two teachers also occasionally taught together or impersonated historical figures or famous artists.

The proximity of mentor and beginning teacher classrooms was also found to be a positive factor in successful mentoring relationships. The teachers can easily talk for a few minutes between classes or before or after school. Being on separate floors, in separate buildings, or even at opposite ends of a hallway can mean that mentor and beginning teacher see each other less often and thereby have fewer opportunities for conversation.

An age difference of eight to fifteen years is recommended so that the mentor is viewed as experienced. The age difference may be important even for nontraditional beginning teachers. Often a veteran teacher will expect an older beginning teacher to be more knowledgeable and may occasionally forget that he or she—no matter what age—is inexperienced. The disparity should not be so wide, however, that a parenting relationship develops. Sometimes, too, age differences can be generational differences. Hank Karp, Connie Fuller, and Danilo Sirias (2002) state that "boomers bring to the table experience, a sense of group values, and a long-term perspective. Xers bring a focus on the present, a high-tech proficiency, and a balanced view of life and work." When ages vary considerably, the mentor pair need to appreciate their differences rather than seek similarities. In addition, while age is significant, the maturity levels of the participants are even more important.

On the issue of gender, several research studies have implied that same-gender mentoring relationships may be more professionally compatible. These studies also suggest that men and women think differently and approach teaching in different ways (Graham 1993, Niday 1996).

Wayne and Eileen watched as their colleagues, Kris and Dan, stood up to explain gender differences. Kris said, "During my student teaching, I had a female cooperating teacher and a female university supervisor. We had conferences in which they just let me talk things through. When I came here as a first-year teacher several years ago, Dan was assigned to me as my mentor." Kris turned and smiled at Dan. She said, "Dan is more of a 'suggestions and fix-it' kind of person."

The teachers turned to look at Dan, who returned Kris's smile.

Kris continued, "You can call me a sexist, call me a generalist"—Dan's laughter interrupted her—"but I think that men want to know what the problem is and they want to fix it." Dan smiled at the crowd and nodded. Eileen and Wayne could tell that gender was a topic the two had discussed at length.

Grinning, Kris explained, "During our conferences, I knew that Dan would ask me what problems I had, and he didn't want me to ramble. He wanted me to tell him a problem so he could fix it. Before each conference, I would think about what topic I wanted to discuss. Then, on my way to school, I would rehearse how I would describe it to Dan."

Kris handed the microphone to Dan, who explained, "I guess we did come at problems differently. But I changed, too. Sometimes I decided she didn't want my advice. She just wanted somebody to listen. So I listened, and sometimes I asked questions, and nine times out of ten she would come up with her own solution to whatever was bothering her." He watched as Kris nodded. "It might be better for mentors to be the same gender, but Kris and I talked about it." He smiled, "In fact, we talked about it a lot. We just needed to hear that we come at and settle problems differently."

As Kris and Dan returned to their seats, Wayne turned to Eileen. "I guess since I'll be mentoring a female teacher, I should think about gender. I just thought being a mentor meant that I would give advice and save her from all her problems."

Eileen nodded. "And I learned that if a male beginning teacher asks for my advice, I should listen and ask questions to help him solve his own problems."

The differences in thinking and talking observed by Kris and Dan parallel what Deborah Tannen (2007) refers to as the male use of "report-talk" and the female use of "rapport-talk." Although Kris and Dan developed a successful mentoring relationship, they might have felt more comfortable in one that encouraged and built on their own way of thinking. A same-gender match is also less likely to cause unnecessary concern that the relationship has moved from the professional to the personal (see Chapter 13).

We have observed many mixed-gender mentoring relationships that have been extremely successful. More than age, gender, or any other factor, individual personalities are the key to creating and sustaining effective professional relationships. Enthusiasm, trustworthiness, adaptability, and good listening skills are often the hallmarks of mentoring success. Ellen Moir, Janet Gless, and Wendy Baron advise that the mentor has "strong interpersonal skills, credibility with peers and administrators, a demonstrated curiosity and eagerness to learn, respect for multiple perspectives, and outstanding instructional practice" (1999, 112–113).

✄ · Mentoring Tensions · ✄

Eileen leaned over to Wayne. "I liked hearing about the best combinations between mentors and beginning teachers."

Wayne nodded. "I did, too. I also liked hearing about how to make a not-so-good match into a better one."

"Me, too. I like the success stories." Eileen hesitated. "But the next part is on 'mentoring tensions.' That sounds pretty negative."

"Oh, but the speaker is Larry. He's always telling stories in the teacher lounge. I bet he has a lot of good examples."

Despite the numerous positive benefits of mentoring, tension can arise in a mentoring relationship.

- Lack of time for collegial conversations.
- Philosophical differences between mentor and beginning teacher.
- Failure to separate mentoring from evaluation.
- Inappropriate length of relationship.

The most common problem in mentoring relationships is a lack of time for collegial conversations. When a beginning teacher and mentor do not have a scheduled time to meet, it inevitably weakens the relationship. For instance, Elizabeth, a beginning teacher who was also a swimming coach, said she had to be at practices before and after school and often on Saturdays. Since she and Kerry, her mentor, did not share the same preparation period or the same lunch period, they could meet for only a few minutes between classes or in the evening. This situation made conversation nearly impossible and compromised their mentoring relationship. Kerry told a friend, "She hasn't requested time [to see me], but I think part of it is that she's so in the thick of it. You know, it's called, 'Do I plan or do I call and talk to my mentor about planning?' " (Niday 1996).

School districts can help resolve the time issue by introducing innovative reforms. In the business world, new employees usually have fewer responsibilities, but in education, novices are expected to shoulder as much work as more experienced teachers. Fewer students or fewer classes would allow the new teacher to ease into the profession and have more time for reflection and for mentoring conferences.

The school district could also encourage quality mentoring by occasionally hiring substitute teachers, giving the two teachers time to confer, plan, view teaching videotapes, and reflect. Making time available for inservices would allow mentors to learn mentoring strategies. Meeting with other mentors in the building to share techniques could also be helpful; beginning teachers also appreciate meeting with their peers and talking about their successes and concerns. If the school district cannot allot sufficient time for mentoring relationships to develop to their full potential, teachers can turn to alternative formats such as a dialogue journal or email.

Differences in educational philosophies can create barriers between the beginning teacher and the mentor (Sullivan 2004). Dissonance occasionally encourages both to consider another perspective, but if the two participants do not agree on basic teaching beliefs, they may have to work hard to remain open-minded and find common ground. The following example (Niday 1996) suggests how two different philosophies might coexist in the same classroom:

> When Nancy entered Sheila's classroom as a student teacher, she immediately noted Sheila's use of lectures and worksheets. Recognizing her own desire to provide a student-centered atmosphere, Nancy wrote about her concerns in her journal, planning on paper her approach to overcome what at first seemed to be a formidable obstacle. She began teaching the study skills unit using the traditional workbook approach and received Sheila's laudatory comments. Then, after only a few days, she slowly veered away from the workbook and inserted her own ideas. First she had students turn to work with a partner. When Sheila

commented upon the success of the lesson, Nancy felt comfortable in launching into small-group work.

Both participants recognized and accepted their differences. Nancy wrote in her journal, "To have the chairs screech and move around and have them work in groups, I think, appeals more to me than it does to her." Similarly, Sheila acknowledged to her colleagues, "I think she does a better job of not being so teacher-oriented as I am . . . I tend to be more of the central figure. I think she comes at it wanting them to discover, to learn on their own . . . she wants the students to experience."

Even though Nancy's and Sheila's philosophies and strategies differed, they talked about and accepted each other's differences. As the semester progressed, Sheila started replacing worksheets with large-group and small-group discussions and shifted from being a "guide" to being "guided" into new ways of thinking. By adopting an open-minded stance, Sheila discovered that she, too, could be a learner.

A third tension can arise over the issue of evaluation. Researchers studying the mentoring of teachers tend to encourage separating mentoring and evaluation (Bey and Holmes 1992). Beginning teachers may well hesitate to approach their mentors with problems if they are aware that these same mentors will later evaluate their performance. Similarly, mentors may find it difficult to be objective in evaluating beginning teachers for whom they feel empathy. Requiring mentors to evaluate their new colleagues creates a conflict between the involvement required for nurturing and the objectivity required for judging. Ideally, beginning teachers should be free to view their mentors as guides, thinkers, and coaches.

The following example illustrates the difficulties of trying to play the dual roles of mentor and evaluator.

José, the science department chair in a large inner-city school, viewed it as his duty to mentor a new science faculty member. He and Victor, a twenty-two-year-old university graduate, launched into an effective mentoring relationship, eagerly sharing their ideas. After a few weeks of school, José informed Victor that as a department chair, he would observe and evaluate Victor's teaching. In a preconference to the observation, Victor described his unit on seed germination, which included an array of experiments.

On the observation day, Victor erroneously assumed that in order for José to see him "teaching" he would need to be the primary participant. Therefore, he shifted his class discussion to a lecture and his student experiments to a teacher demonstration. José observed a "one-person show." Assuming that this was a typical class, he gave Victor low ratings on the evaluation instrument. When Victor saw his points and heard José's observational analysis, his teaching confidence plunged. Suddenly his mentor and confidant had become an authority figure. To whom could he turn for guidance? At a time when he most needed mentoring, he realized that his chief problem concerned his mentor.

Not surprisingly, almost all mentor studies advise separating mentoring and evaluation. Mentors find it difficult to establish a close relationship with a beginning teacher and then suddenly distance themselves to perform the evaluator role. Once José surmised that Victor now seemed leery about sharing classroom problems, José approached his principal and asked him to take over the formal evaluation so that José could return to his role as a true mentor.

One of the most difficult experiences for first-year teachers is an administrator's observation and evaluation of their teaching. Administrators often offer constructive criticism, aware of the need to encourage continued growth in every teacher, especially the beginning teacher. But mentors also need to be aware that even constructive comments at this early stage can shatter the confidence of the beginning teacher. They may want to provide encouragement prior to the administrator's evaluation and support afterward. Sometimes mentors merely need to reinforce a fact often overlooked by a sensitive beginning teacher: that the evaluator's listing of their strengths usually far exceeds any suggestions for improvement. By helping novice teachers put these comments in perspective, mentors focus their attention on the larger picture—student learning and professional teacher growth.

Confidentiality is an important trust connection between the mentor and beginning teacher. For instance, if the beginning teacher is arriving to school a few minutes late each day, the mentor needs to ask the reason for the tardiness and then explain the need for professionalism. The mentor should resolve the situation quickly and not inform an administrator. This action will ensure that the trust is maintained between mentor and beginning teacher and that mentoring and evaluation are separated.

A fourth source of tension, the length of a mentoring relationship, can either diminish or prolong a novice teacher's dependent stage. Mary Lou's mentor, Daren, decided that she no longer needed his assistance after he had observed her initial successes, but Mary Lou still felt a need for support for her work and discussion of her teaching practices. In contrast, Erin, as a beginning teacher, felt "mothered and smothered" by Vicki's constant attention. A fine balance exists among dependence, independence, and interdependence. Although "beginning" teachers are described as being in their first, second, or third year, the ideal mentoring relationship encourages beginning teachers to become progressively more independent and self-reliant. In the most productive relationships, mentors gradually withdraw as beginning teachers gain experience and move from being dependent learners to being colleagues who enjoy collaboration but no longer require day-to-day reassurance.

> Eileen whispered, "Hey, you were right, Wayne. Larry did have some great examples."
>
> Wayne nodded. "And now I know it's not good to be both a mentor and an evaluator. I think that was the problem last year when Maggie was mentoring Janie. As the department chair, she was trying to do both jobs."
>
> "And Janie ended up leaving our school. I hear she's going back to get a business degree. It's too bad she left teaching."
>
> "I'm glad our principal said she would evaluate new faculty members from now on. That makes more sense."
>
> Eileen nodded as she scanned the agenda. "Next we're going to discuss team mentoring. That sounds like fun. I like the idea that this will be a shared responsibility."

✎ · Working with Team Mentors · ✎

The 2005 National Commission on Teaching and America's Future report titled "Induction into Learning Communities" recommends team mentoring. "Unless we move beyond the traditional one-to-one mentoring model, we will continue to reinforce the industrial-era practice of stand-alone teaching in isolated classrooms" (1). The commission advocates a team approach, using "strong professional communities" (3) and "a network of supports, people, and processes that are all focused on assuring that novices become effective in their work" (4). The commission members show a change in philosophy over the centuries, saying, "We present induction viewed from the perspective of its role in the dominant culture of teaching and learning, from the 19th century 'factory era' to the 20th century culture of solo teaching, to a transformative 21st century model in which new teachers become part of a community of learners" (6). In their six recommendations for improving mentoring (9), team mentoring is second:

- Mentoring is just one part of full induction system.
- Mentors and novices work in teams.

- Mentors are selected for skill in content, pedagogy, and ability to coach and work with other teachers.

- Extensive, continuous training for mentors.

- Structured time and incentives for mentors (e.g., stipends, planning time, professional credits, and advancement).

- Clear expectations and accountability of mentors.

Since many elementary school teachers work in grade-level teams, many middle schools use interdisciplinary teams, and high schools tend to operate in departmental units, it may be advantageous for a beginning teacher to work with team mentors. This gives the beginning teachers multiple perspectives to situations, allowing the mentee to see different options and select the one that best meets her own teaching style.

Team mentoring also allows each mentor to use specific talents. For instance, Paula's talent may lie in classroom management; Quinn, parental conferences; Jeanne, long-range planning; Barry, critical thinking; and Karin, assessment. Others might have expertise in organization, creativity, or differentiated learning. By meeting with a specific person, the beginning teacher may feel more comfortable asking about a specific area and taking only small amounts of time from each mentor.

Another advantage to team mentoring is that a mentor is usually available when a beginning teacher wants assistance. For example, if Maryann is thinking about today's group project reports and wonders what to do if some group members are absent, she might discover that Nancy is in a meeting, Chris has before-school swimming practice, and Irene is printing copies, but since Barry is free, she can ask him her question. Maryann may feel less constrained in requesting assistance of a mentor since she won't need to worry about taking so much of his or her time.

In addition, during team meetings, the team can ask if the beginning teacher has specific questions or concerns. Also during a team meeting, the team can plan an interdisciplinary unit together, illustrating the planning process and asking the beginning teacher for ideas, making her feel like a vital member of the group. (See Chapter 4 for an example of an interdisciplinary team planning session.)

On the other hand, team mentoring does carry some disadvantages. Sometimes different mentors offer a variety of planning methods, instructional strategies, and teaching philosophies, which might confuse or overwhelm a beginning teacher. This is especially true in a student-teaching situation when a student teacher often feels he has to vary his teaching style in each cooperating teacher's classroom.

Another problem sometimes occurs when each mentor thinks that the other mentors are giving support when perhaps none of the mentors are asking the beginning teacher if she has concerns or questions. Other times they may be merely asking lightly, "So, how are things going?" and accepting a general response of "Fine" rather than probing more deeply and having longer, sustained conferences.

Despite these possible drawbacks, team mentoring holds many possibilities for enriching the mentoring situation. If team mentors discuss and analyze the previously stated potential hindrances and find ways to counter them, then the mentoring situation can be strengthened for all participants.

> Eileen looked at Wayne. "I like the team approach. What do you think, Wayne?"
>
> Wayne smiled. "The more help the better! It looks as if we're going to talk about working with university supervisors and school administrators next."

✉ · Working with the University Supervisor · ✉

Who is the mentor's mentor? Usually a third party, the university supervisor, provides support to the beginning teacher and to the mentor. Although traditionally university supervisors have worked primarily with student teachers, increasingly they also work with and support first- or second-year teachers. Sometimes mentors feel threatened by the university supervisor's visits, yet while it is true that most university supervisors are required to evaluate the new teacher, their role is one of offering assistance, professional friendship, and support. As seasoned professional educators, university supervisors can be an invaluable objective set of eyes to watch what is happening in the beginning teacher's classroom and to offer guidance to the teacher and the mentor.

The university supervisor is one of the three players on a team that also includes the beginning teacher and the mentor. A three-way exchange of phone numbers and email addresses may be helpful to encourage communication. Mentors should feel comfortable in communicating with the university supervisor about a student's successes, as well as their own questions and concerns. The mentor and the university supervisor play similar roles, encouraging, nudging, and modeling. Together, the two can provide collegial discussions and reflective thinking to make the beginning teaching experience enriching for all three participants.

∞ · Working with School Administrators · ∞

A school administrator can also serve as the mentor's mentor and as a secondary mentor to the beginning teacher. Mentors will want to model and encourage a good working relationship with administrators.

In introducing the student teacher to a school administrator, mentors might enhance the relationship by talking about the student teacher's areas of special interest. Some principals choose to meet with all the student teachers in the school after the semester has begun to share background information about the school's mission, teacher expectations, and student population and to participate in an informal question-and-answer exchange. The mentor can ask the student teacher to share any new insights gained from this meeting.

As the semester progresses, if a student teacher is ready, mentors might encourage inviting an administrator to observe one or more lessons. This helps to prepare student teachers for the more formal evaluation they will encounter as beginning teachers. As can be expected, beginning teachers may be quite nervous about formal evaluations. Preobservation conferences with the principal and a separate conference with their mentor can help dispel fears by allowing time to discuss the procedures followed during the observation. Seeing the evaluation instrument beforehand can also ease initial anxieties. For instance, if the administrator states an intent to use scripting by jotting down the teachers' and students' responses, then the student teacher will not be surprised to see the administrator writing lengthy notes.

Administrators may also volunteer to discuss the job application process with student teachers and to peruse and offer advice about a résumé, cover letter, and teaching portfolio. Some administrators have provided mock interviews or discussed the type of questions usually asked during a team interview. Others may be willing to write a letter of recommendation. Mentors should encourage student teachers to initiate conversations with the school administrator and form a good working relationship.

Mentors can initiate a good relationship between the beginning teacher and the administrator by discussing effective administrator relationships during initial mentoring sessions. Principals usually set aside a special meeting or inservice day to acquaint new faculty members with the school district's policies and expectations. The principal usually issues an open invitation for further one-on-one conversations when more questions arise, thereby offering a secondary mentorship to beginning teachers.

The school administrator and the beginning teacher will have direct contact during the formal evaluation. As mentioned previously, the mentor should wisely separate mentoring from evaluation and serve a supporting, not an assessing, role. During the principal's formal evaluation, the mentor may wish to assume the stance of encourager and listener, both prior to the evaluation and following the observation and postconference review. The formal evaluation is an opportunity to list teaching strengths and goals. Lortie (1975) talks about the need for beginning teachers to receive "authoritative reassurance" (147). The mentor serves as the collegial guide and coach; the school administrator provides the "authoritative reassurance."

Administrators will, of course, wish to seek other opportunities to strengthen their relationships with beginning teachers. For those working on a mentoring team with a school administrator, the following suggestions might be helpful to principals, or even to interdisciplinary team members or curriculum specialists, as they work together with their new colleagues.

- Use the beginning teacher's first name frequently to show your acceptance of the new faculty member.

- To avoid general conversations of the "How are things going?"/"Fine" variety, ask specific, authentic questions, such as, "Are you finding that the students have the computer experience you expected?"

- Involve the new faculty member: For instance, new university graduates often have current technology expertise and may be willing to talk about or demonstrate particular programs or equipment. This involvement will increase the beginning teacher's confidence and sense of belonging in the school.

- Inquire of the beginning teacher, "What questions would you like to ask?" Beginning teachers, like students, are often afraid to ask questions. They usually welcome opportunities to learn.

(See Chapter 11 for more information about the mentor-administrator relationship.)

Wayne turned to his colleague. "Wow, I didn't know there was so much to this mentoring job."

"It does sound like a lot to know," Eileen agreed, "but somehow it's reassuring to learn about what is involved and how to do a better job."

"You're right," Wayne answered, rubbing his mustache. "When the principal asked me to mentor Karla this year, I just took it as one more job to do. Now I can see that it's an important responsibility. After this inservice, I'm going to take this job more seriously."

"OK, Wayne," Eileen said, "just don't go overboard with the serious part. We also need to show these beginning teachers that teaching can be rewarding—even fun!" She thought for a moment. "Maybe as mentors we can help each other this year."

Wayne grinned. "It's a deal."

⤜ · Summary · ⤛

Mentoring relationships tend to be highly complex. Listening, talking, and asking questions can often resolve potential difficulties. Factors that enhance mentoring relationships include a mentor's extensive teaching experience, shared content areas or grade levels, physical proximity of the classroom, and an age variance between the older mentor and younger teacher. Factors that may inhibit mentoring relationships include lack of time, differences in philosophical beliefs, failure to separate mentoring from evaluation, and an inappropriately long mentoring relationship. By working alongside team members, the university supervisor, and school administrators, mentors can ensure that beginning teachers will have a positive balance of collaboration and independence. By recognizing the complexities in mentoring, we can view collegial relationships as ongoing, reciprocal, and active forms of professional growth.

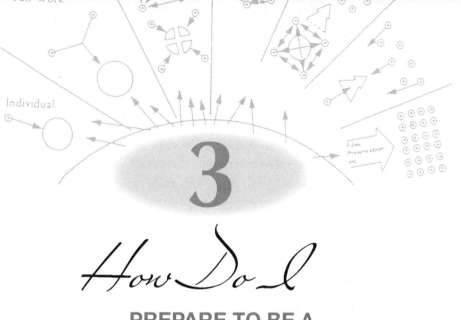

3

How Do I

PREPARE TO BE A
MENTORING GUIDE?

The true aim of everyone who aspires to be a teacher should be,
not to impart his own opinion, but to kindle minds.

—Frederick W. Robertson, *Dear Teacher* (Paul C. Brownlow, ed.)

Listening or telling? Questioning or critiquing? Mentoring or managing? These are the questions that you, as a mentor, might ponder as you start working with a beginning teacher. Now that we have discussed the various benefits of mentoring, we can explore ways to make this teaching experience productive.

First, you might wish to think about your philosophical beliefs and the responsibilities involved in mentoring. Traditionally, mentors have been the "experts" who pass on to beginning teachers the "tricks of the trade" that they have learned over the years. This is the "I'll tell you what not to do so you do not make the same errors I did" philosophy. But just as this approach often does not work for parents, it may not work for mentors. An alternative to the "telling" approach is the strategy of guiding, reflecting, and coaching. The *Oxford English Dictionary* (*OED*) traces the origin of the word mentor to Homer's *The Odyssey*, in which Mentor served as a guide and advisor of Odysseus's son, Telemachus. According to the *OED*, the name may derive from a base word meaning "remember, think, or counsel," and it gives as the definition "an experienced and trusted advisor or guide, a teacher, a tutor."

In the past, mentoring roles might have involved advising. More recently, however, the mentor's role has been one of listening, questioning, and encouraging reflective thinking (Schön 1983, 1987, 1991). Perhaps Frederick W. Robertson's comment at the beginning of this chapter (Brownlow 1995) could be changed from "teacher" to "mentor": "The true aim of everyone who aspires to be a mentor should be, not to impart his own opinion, but to kindle minds." Teachers try to be student centered; mentors attempt to help beginning teachers analyze their classroom practice and think about what they do in the classroom and why. By serving as guides, mentors can point beginning teachers in creative directions so they can discover how to develop effective student learning conditions.

✐ · Welcoming the Beginning Teacher · ✐

Once you have accepted the role of mentor, consider ways of creating a welcoming environment. Your initial reception may play a key role in how your young colleagues perceive themselves as teachers. Effective mentoring, like effective lesson planning, begins long before the bell rings. The following is a list of questions you may wish to consider as you prepare for the arrival of the beginning teacher:

- How can I help the new teacher learn about the culture of this school?

- How can I assist the new teacher in developing rapport with students?

- What suggestions can I make and what approaches can I model for proactive class-room management?

- What strategies can I suggest to help the new teacher win the respect of students and colleagues?

You may wish to arrange an informal meeting with the beginning teacher before her first day at school. This meeting may be an ideal time to discuss the educational mission statement of the department or school district, various policies and procedures, and curricula. If you have been asked to mentor a student teacher, you and your principal, along with your department chair or team leader, may wish to set up an interview to ask the student teacher about her background, beliefs, and goals (see Appendix for possible interview questions). This exchange of information will help participants determine whether the placement will be a productive one for both the mentor and the student teacher.

Acclimating to the Environment

There are many possible ways of helping the beginning teacher become acclimated to the school environment. Consider these examples.

> As a member of the English Department, Sally, a seventh-grade teacher, participated in interviewing and hiring Beth Warren, a recent graduate of a university teacher education program, to teach eighth-grade English the following year. Sally also volunteered to serve as Beth's mentor in the transition from the university to the middle school. To help Beth earn respect from her prospective eighth graders, Sally told her seventh graders about the projects ahead next year, in the eighth-grade curriculum. She went on to describe Beth Warren and her enthusiasm for teaching and asked the seventh graders to write a letter to Ms. Warren telling her about their interests. Finally, she took each student's photograph and taped it to the student's letter.
>
> Over the summer, Beth read all the letters and matched students' faces with their names and interests. When the eighth graders entered the classroom that fall, Beth stood at the door and greeted each of them by name: "Hi, you must be Jeremy. I'm Ms. Warren. How did your baseball team do this summer?" Sally's idea, sending on information about the students, helped Beth become an insider from the first moment of the school year. Later, Beth passed out letters she had written to each student commenting on individual interests. This well-planned preparation and exchange established an atmosphere of mutual respect that promised a productive year.

By linking the photos and letters, Sally prepared Beth to meet her students with confidence. Because Beth had taken time to learn their names and something about each of them, students realized that Beth valued them and their time together in the classroom.

Sally also thought of ways to make the faculty environment easier for Beth. She loaned Beth the latest school yearbook so that she could learn the names and faces of the faculty, the secretaries, and the custodial staff. In addition, Sally put together a "beginning teacher" packet that included a map of the school, tips on parent/teacher conferences, and information on various school policies.

Frank wanted to aid Jennifer's transition into student teaching. During the fall semester, when one of his fourth graders asked about a special project, Frank replied, "That will work better when we have two teachers in the classroom. Once Ms. Smith arrives, we can try out that project." This strategy helped to establish a welcoming environment and increased students' enthusiasm for Ms. Smith's arrival.

On Jennifer's first day, the students observed two equally sized teachers' desks placed at equal positions in the classroom. Frank introduced Jennifer by saying, "Ms. Smith will be joining me in teaching you this semester." Presented to the class as an equal (a "teacher" rather than "student teacher"), and given a desk of her own, Jennifer felt welcomed into the profession. These gestures might appear minor, but they contribute greatly to the student teacher's overall self-esteem. They also signal students that their new teacher deserves their attention and respect.

Later in the day, Frank and Jennifer team taught, and Jennifer gave directions for small-group work. Frank had already asked the students to make name tags for their desks. Looking directly at students and calling them by name, Jennifer quickly placed students into each group. As the groups worked, she walked around the room, again addressing each child by name to help her associate the name with the face. This technique headed off classroom management challenges. The students quickly understood that to Jennifer they were not anonymous individuals. They followed Frank's lead and saw the two as "my teachers" rather than "my teacher and his student teacher." They seemed to sense the cooperative relationship between the two.

Frank's strategies recognized the importance of immediately involving Jennifer in the life of the classroom. His actions helped her feel at ease and indicated her shared role to the students. Other ways to involve the student teacher at once include taking attendance, giving announcements, or handing out writing folders. These actions set the tone for the student teacher's active participation in the class.

Unfortunately, such preplanning techniques may not always be possible. Here, a teacher attempts mentoring without the advantage of preplanning.

Maggie, a middle school vocal teacher, volunteered to mentor Juanita, a middle school instrumental music teacher. Maggie wanted Juanita to get off to a good start, but problems abounded. Since the previous year's instrumental music teacher had quit at the end of the school year, there was no way to prepare students for a new teacher. Also, Juanita would be teaching hundreds of students, and Maggie worried about how she would become acquainted with each one. She decided to lend Juanita her camera to take photos of small groups of students with their instruments during band lessons.

In addition, Maggie made comments to her own music students that show how she valued her new colleague. She told a quartet that Juanita might play a flute solo to introduce their song "because I heard that Ms. Chavez is a great flutist." Another time she suggested, "Maybe Ms. Chavez would loan us some percussion players for this number." By speaking of Juanita in a positive, professional way, Maggie modeled the respect she wanted the students to adopt toward her new colleague.

Later in the semester, when Juanita mentioned management problems in working with over one hundred students simultaneously, Maggie offered to observe one of her orchestra sessions. Maggie slipped unobtrusively into the back of the room after the class period had started. She observed but never intervened, not wishing to compromise Juanita's authority. Later, the two teachers discussed ways to establish an atmosphere of respect in the class.

While these planning and mentoring techniques may not be identical to your own specific situation, these examples are intended to provide you with some ideas for approaching your interactions with a beginning teacher more productively. Consider strategies that help the beginning teacher feel like a professional. Find ways to foster respect for the new teacher in the classroom.

Here are a few simple preparations you might consider in welcoming new teachers:

- Stock the beginning teacher's desk with supplies, such as a stapler, tape dispenser, paper clips, notepads, pens, and other necessities. She will appreciate not having to make repeated trips to the office for supplies.

- Compile a teacher notebook of helpful materials—a school map, a personnel list, a note on school regulations, class lists, schedule of classes, and so on.

- Consider ways to assist the beginning teacher in learning students' names—seating charts, photos, yearbooks, written papers, "getting to know you" bulletin boards.

Mentors can use many ways to help acclimate beginning teachers to the school environment, including helping them become aware of the school culture (see Chapter 8).

Establishing a Relationship That Builds Trust

A key factor in any productive mentoring relationship is mutual trust. The following list provides strategies to encourage working relationships based on trust:

- Write a personal letter of welcome to the beginning teacher. Even if you have met in person and are communicating by phone or email, a handwritten note describing your excitement about the upcoming experience will be especially valued. Sometimes beginning teachers think of themselves as burdens instead of assets, so express your enthusiasm about their arrival.

- Consider inviting your new colleague to a "getting-to-know-you" session to

  1. Discuss courses and other curricular interests, extracurricular activities, school communities, duty schedules, the school calendar, and so on.

  2. Tour the building, including administrative offices, the supply room, faculty restrooms, the cafeteria and commons, the media center, teacher lounge, and other areas.

  3. Show the teacher where equipment is located, including the photocopier, computers, and audio-visual equipment.

  4. Introduce the new teacher to other colleagues, such as the administrators, other teaching colleagues, secretaries, custodians, and support staff.

- Share your own philosophy of teaching, classroom management, and assessment. Ask the beginning teacher to share hers (teacher education classes often include a writing assignment on educational philosophy). Discuss the similarities and differences in your views. Ask open-ended questions:

  When did you know you wanted to be a teacher?

  What gifts do you think you bring to teaching?

  What successes have you experienced in your teacher preparation program?

  What books have been especially helpful to you in preparing to become a teacher?

Planning, Teaching, and Researching Collaboratively

Collaboration is an important way to strengthen the performance of a new teacher. Among many possible avenues for collaborative work, consider the following:

- Plan a unit together. Whether the beginning teacher works in your classroom or down the hall, try planning a unit together to explore the benefits of collaboration. To ensure that the beginning teacher has an equal role in the planning, you might wish to work with subject material that is new to both of you.

- Teach a unit together. Instead of giving the beginning teacher a preplanned unit, suggest that you coteach a jointly planned unit. You could combine your two classes for that particular unit and pair your students to enhance learning. Alternate your leadership roles: one teacher might conduct an introductory motivational activity for the unit, and the other might give an overview, providing a rationale and briefly describing related activities and assessments. One teacher might give directions for the first activity, and then together both teachers could monitor small-group work. Or one teacher could encourage class brainstorming while the other writes the ideas on the overhead projector.

  In a science class, you might jointly conduct an experiment, with one teacher demonstrating the procedures and the other leading a class discussion, predicting the outcome or analyzing the results. For student teachers, team teaching provides a gentle entry into teaching; for you as mentor, the experience can help you decide if the student teacher is ready to plan and teach independently. For first-year teachers, this approach also builds confidence.

- Share mini-activities such as reading aloud or role playing. Combine your classes and collaboratively enact scenes from a story. If students are to give a presentation, the two of you might model the "do" and "don't" principles of speaking and using a visual aid. For a history class, you might play the parts of two historical figures considering political strategies or negotiations.

- Participate in a joint action inquiry. If a few male students in each classroom seem to be dominating class discussions, for example, develop several research questions: What is the significance of gender domination in class discussions? In what ways do quiet students tend to participate in discussions? Which methods encourage or discourage participation? A class-based action inquiry changes the tone of the dialogue between new and experienced teachers by making them research partners rather than critic and criticized. Using this method, you can often transform problems into opportunities for reflection and productive action.

  Following this discussion, you might try observing each other's classroom and documenting what students do during discussion. For instance, one teacher might "script" (write down word-for-word) the discussion questions, the other teacher's responses to students, or questions from students in the class. It would also be helpful to display this information on a chart. The chart might note gender, the areas of the room where most discussion originates, the number of responses per student, and other ways of looking at teaching and learning (see Chapter 5). Once these data have been collected, the two of you can brainstorm ways to increase student success. The beginning teacher will probably appreciate the mentor's willingness to work with her toward a solution.

- Use tape recorders as journals or research tools. If you find it difficult to write in a journal, you might try taping your comments and questions to each other. If you commute alone to school, you might try keeping a journal by talking aloud while you drive, recording your thoughts on tape. Then you can exchange tapes.

  You might also try tape-recording a class session. A tape recorder can't capture everything that happens in the classroom, but you can listen to yourself giving directions, to student discussions in small or large groups, and to your questioning and feedback strategies. By focusing on a specific area, such as gender participation, you can distance yourself and see your classroom more objectively. By sharing tapes with the beginning teacher, both teachers learn about each other's strategies. For instance, if you are both fourth-grade teachers teaching the same unit on pioneers to different students, you can discover new techniques and perspectives. What is most important is the two-way exchange that shows you value the creative ideas a new teacher brings to the classroom.

- Invite the beginning teacher to observe your classroom. If the new teacher's planning period doesn't coincide with your class time, ask another teacher to substitute in the beginning teacher's classroom during this time. If you're in a team mentoring situation, invite the beginning teacher to observe each of the team members as they teach. Each team member can substitute one period in the beginning teacher's classroom to allow for these observations.

- Observe the beginning teacher's class (if the school district has an induction requirement, this may be a requirement). In team mentoring situations, the team might give the beginning teacher a choice of multiple observations by several team members or only one team member, giving the new teacher a voice in a personal comfort zone and learning style.

❧ · Providing Freedom to Experiment · ❧

Even though beginning teachers may appear to be confident, they often need—and want—feedback. A reassuring comment might simply be, "You are at or ahead of where you should be at this time in your student teaching/first year of teaching. I'm extremely pleased with your progress." This tells new teachers that, while more growth is expected, current growth is on track.

Many mentors simply hand beginning teachers ready-made lesson plans or units that have proved successful, but new teachers need more challenging opportunities. Although most new teachers are capable adults, they are still novices at teaching. They should be allowed to stumble occasionally while they learn.

> Molly asked Katie, her first-grade student teacher, "Are you prepared for today's lesson?" Katie nodded eagerly. Molly noticed that the mural paper wasn't cut and the markers hadn't been sorted into baskets for small-group work. "Do you have all the materials ready?" Again Katie nodded.
>
> Molly mulled over whether or not she should intercede. Since Katie was at the beginning of her student teaching, Molly decided that it was important to uphold Katie's confidence with a successful experience. "Do you have the materials ready for the small-group work?" she prodded. With the additional questioning, Katie recognized where she might falter in her lesson. Molly asked her, "What do you think would have happened in the classroom if you had stopped the lesson to take time to prepare the materials for the groups?"
>
> Katie thought a moment. "I guess first graders don't have long attention spans. They might not have been patient waiting for me to cut the paper and sort the markers. They probably would have started talking and moving around." Molly's questions helped Katie see not only the "what" of the situation but also the "why."

You will probably want to offer suggestions to prevent a complete failure in the classroom, but it is even better to ask questions that assist the beginning teacher toward her own conclusions. Freedom to experiment and take risks is essential to developing independence.

We can view the initial teaching experience in two ways, as evaluation or as empowerment. An authoritarian mentoring stance can turn this time into a "sink or swim" experience. The mentor, in effect, says, "Prove yourself. I'm watching you." A collaborative mentoring stance, in contrast, establishes an atmosphere of "I value you and want to help you improve." The mentor can adopt an attitude of "You're on your own, and you'll have to show me your worthiness as a teacher" or an attitude of "We'll work together to help you succeed." Ideally, the mentor's words and actions convey a collaborative stance.

Knowing when to step in and when to step back can be difficult. As a mentor, you may have to determine whether to caution the beginning teacher against certain procedures or give her permission to try new strategies and perhaps fail.

> Penny, a first-year second-grade teacher, planned a cookie-making venture for her students. Excited about the possibilities of making the project interdisciplinary, she told her mentor, Gineen, that she wanted to teach fraction skills while students

were measuring the ingredients and explain the purposes of butter and flour while students were stirring the mixture. In addition, she planned to use the cookies to celebrate a cultural holiday. Afterwards she envisioned having the students compile a class booklet of writings and drawings about the cookie-making experience. Though Penny talked enthusiastically about the project, her mentor wrote in her own teaching journal, "It's a great idea, but I don't think she realizes how complex the task will be for second graders."

On the cookie-baking day, Penny started the project by circulating among four groups of second graders, dispensing utensils and ingredients. Her plans quickly changed as problems arose. First, several groups spattered the mixture over the floor, and Penny substituted stirring instructions for the math lesson. Then the science lesson disappeared as Penny saw how slowly the children measured each ingredient. As the clock ticked closer to lunchtime, Penny realized that most of them had never spooned cookie dough onto baking sheets, and she watched in dismay as several groups placed huge globs of dough in the middle. Seeing her carefully planned lesson turn chaotic, Penny raced from group to group, frantically providing more directions and demonstrations.

At this moment, her mentor looked in, and Penny came toward her pleading, "Could you help me?" Together the two teachers demonstrated cookie spooning procedures, and the students took turns. As the bell rang for lunch, Penny surveyed the oven-ready baking sheets, smiled thankfully at her mentor, and breathed a sigh of relief.

Later, during their conference time, Gineen gently asked Penny, "What did you learn from this experience, and what would you do differently?" By this time Penny was able to laugh about the near fiasco. "Next time I won't try so many things at once." Chuckling, she added, "And I'll get aides or parents to help me." Gineen appreciated Penny's recognition of the need to determine what children know and can do before embarking on an ambitious project and the need to seek assistance for hands-on projects. As a mentor, Gineen saw the situation as a way for Penny to learn and develop as a teacher.

If this situation had occurred early in a student teacher's experience, Gineen and Penny might have worked as team teachers. However, rescuing a beginning teacher by jumping in to turn a difficult situation around may be unwise. Beginning teachers usually learn more when they experience the problem before they receive the mentor's comments or assistance. Since this was Penny's first year of teaching, Gineen withheld her advice and allowed Penny to encounter the problems firsthand.

Although it is tempting for a mentor to interrupt a student teacher in the middle of a class to add further directions or offer a great example, it is usually much wiser to let the student teacher find an appropriate solution. Mentor and teacher can discuss the situation later, during a conference time. In Penny's case, she had requested help and appreciated Gineen's assistance.

Mentors of student teachers frequently ask when—or whether—they should leave the room while the student teacher is in charge. Unless specifically prohibited by the university or the school district, it is wise to give competent student teachers full charge of the school day for a minimum of two weeks during the student teaching period (the university supervisor may ask for or recommend even longer periods of solo teaching). Sometimes mentors follow a gradual progression toward leaving the student teacher alone by first working quietly at the desk and then moving outside the classroom door. They might follow this with brief trips to the office or the library. Finally, the mentor may be absent from the classroom from bell to bell. This gradual transition allows the student teacher to feel in control yet offers reassurance to the mentor.

A Master's of Teaching (MAT) program with a year-long internship provides special benefits. According to this model, the intern usually begins by observing and team teaching during the first semester and moves into full-time teaching in the second semester. The mentor and intern often plan and teach collaboratively, which allows for phases of interdependence as well as independence that prepare interns for future collaborative work with grade-level or interdisciplinary teams.

Usually, the mentor can accurately and easily estimate the student teacher's level of readiness and confidence. It is wisest, obviously, to err on the side of caution rather than push student teachers beyond their readiness. In addition, the mentor's first responsibility lies in ensuring the learning of the elementary or secondary students in the classroom. However, a student teaching experience needs to include full charge of the classroom to be a realistic introduction to the teaching life.

✎ · Summary · ✎

How you play your role as a mentor and guide to the beginning teacher often defines her view of what it means to be an educator. The ways in which you welcome the beginning teacher as a fellow professional and team participant may influence her self-perception and increase her acceptance by students. Your efforts in preparing for the beginning teacher—establishing a relationship and building trust, and planning and teaching collaboratively—can ease the transition into the teaching profession. Open communication is a key factor in the success of the mentoring relationship and in the beginning teacher's effectiveness in the classroom.

While it may appear that mentoring a beginning teacher requires considerable time and energy, the rewards merit the commitment. Beginning teachers will value your willingness to share your enthusiasm and to provide them with learning opportunities. Although tensions and struggles may arise in the mentoring experience, these concerns are usually outweighed by the positive experiences of both participants.

We began this chapter with the words of Frederick W. Robertson, which suggest that you, the mentor, have the power to kindle the minds not only of your own students but also of the future students the beginning teacher will encounter. While the mentor relationship lasts only a short time, your encouragement as a guiding mentor will be remembered and, indeed, mirrored as the beginning teacher progresses from novice to veteran to mentor teacher.

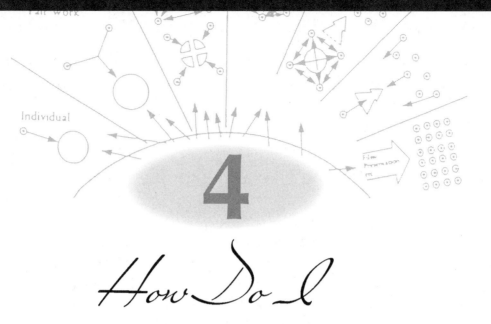

4

How Do I

PREPARE TO BE A MENTORING COACH?

> To coach means to convey a valued colleague
> from where he or she is to where he or she wants to be.

—Arthur L. Costa and Robert J. Garmston, *Cognitive Coaching*

A coach usually sits on the sidelines and provides encouragement and advice to the players on the field. During time-outs, the coach helps the players to see the "big picture" of what is happening on the field.

In a similar way, mentors can coach beginning teachers to connect theory with practice. Arthur Costa and Robert Garmston (2002) advocate "cognitive coaching" as a way for teachers to become conscious of their own teaching practices and philosophies. Rather than use the metaphor of the athletic coach, however, they perceive a coach as a wagon or a vehicle that moves people from one location to another. They encourage goals of trust, mutual learning, and "holonomy," which they define as acting independently and interdependently at the same time, thus assisting teachers to feel at ease in making independent choices while also being able to work cooperatively within a team (3).

Others, such as Barbara Gottesman (2000), refer to peer coaching, one-on-one interchanges in which reciprocal partners learn from each other. Although peer coaching usually involves equally experienced teachers helping each other, it can also encompass mentoring situations, which can become reciprocal learning situations. Both cognitive and peer coaching require you, as the mentor, to think more about your own classroom practice and how students learn.

⋊ · Thinking Like a Mentoring Coach · ⋊

Resisting their perceived role as "experts," mentors have adopted a more collegial stance in their work with less-experienced teachers. Effective mentoring requires a philosophy that encourages questioning, recognizes territoriality, and models continual learning.

Since many educators acknowledge that there are multiple learning and teaching styles, the emphasis has shifted from the "what" of teaching (the many different strategies) to the "why" of teaching ("why" a particular teaching strategy is useful and in what context). You will need to be prepared to describe the "whys" and "hows" of your own practice, even if beginning teachers do not ask you about them directly.

The beginning teacher may observe, or view on videotape, your teaching practices but be unaware of your underlying teaching purposes. You may want to explain, for example, that in order to set a certain tone in the classroom, you emphasize the rule that students must show respect for each other. Or you may wish to describe a quick first-day writing activity you use to learn more about students individually. Similarly, you may need to discuss the rationale for particular teaching practices. Veteran teachers are often naturally intuitive and will choose a particular strategy or select certain materials because "they feel right" or because "I just know they will work." Less-experienced teachers need a more concrete reason for these decisions. As a mentor, you will need to make the implicit explicit by explaining the theory behind your practice.

You also need to realize that beginning teachers can have problems or concerns that are completely unknown to you. New teachers often feel reluctant to question a mentor's classroom practices because they fear their questions will be construed as criticism. It is extremely helpful to state explicitly that the beginning teacher has permission to ask questions and should feel free to do so. You may find these questions surprising or momentarily unsettling, but value them as opportunities for self-analysis and professional growth.

In addition, recognize the territorial nature of classrooms and the school environment. Beginning teachers may hesitate to address their needs, or they may feel uncomfortable in a new school setting. Mentors, especially those working with student teachers, often feel invaded because they share physical space in the room and teaching space in the curriculum. To lessen the problem of shared physical space, you might map out the classroom and talk about "ownership" issues. For instance, Mark, a speech teacher, informed Suzanne, a beginning teacher, "You're welcome to look through my file cabinets at any time and take an extra copy or photocopy something. Just make sure that the files are placed back in alphabetical order so I can find them. Supplies like a stapler and scissors are in this top drawer of my desk in case you need another pair. Otherwise, I'd prefer that you not touch things on top of my desk or in the other desk drawers. I don't have anything too personal here, but I just like my own space. You'll probably feel the same way about your desk, and I'll respect that."

The two also mapped out the curriculum. Mark asked direct questions—"What teaching strategies have worked for you and your students? Are there any areas of teaching that make you feel uncomfortable?"—which allowed Suzanne to admit, "I don't feel that I'm ready to teach debate. Could I observe first and then team teach with you before taking over the course?" Mark's questions promoted open communication that made both more honest and forthcoming in their discussions.

"Curriculum territory" refers to both what is taught and how it is taught. Occasionally a veteran teacher hands a unit folder over to a student teacher, expecting it to be taught without deviation. This, of course, may put the novice teacher at an unfair disadvantage. Allowing beginning teachers the freedom to balance their ideas with yours may force you to see your teaching from a new angle. New teachers often prefer a choice: "Here is the unit I've been using. You're welcome to use whatever is helpful to you, add your own ideas, and discuss your plans with me."

A note of caution: Mentoring conversations occasionally venture into psychological territory by discussing family issues or romantic relationships. We have found that if beginning teachers disclose too much personal information, mentors may view them in a different—sometimes negative—light. We encourage you to treat mentoring as a professional relationship.

Although territoriality implies boundaries, you will also want to display your openness to new ideas and your conviction that learning, including teacher learning, has no boundaries. Whether you are working with a student teacher or a first-year teacher, demonstrate your own active learning. Ask them, "What strategies or materials do you think we should add to this unit?" After a class period in which a student teacher has observed your teaching, you might make a comment such as, "The students didn't seem involved in the discussion I was leading today. What do you think was happening?" By asking the beginning teacher for her opinion and by acknowledging that some days are not, even for you, optimally successful, you can demonstrate how you might pinpoint a weak spot and shift gears next time by trying a different approach. We know from our own mentoring experiences that beginning teachers are more comfortable experimenting when they have watched their mentor review less-than-productive as well as successful practices.

Virginia, a student teacher in English, offered to teach a new novel that had recently been added to the curriculum. Her mentor, Marjorie, gladly accepted, recognizing that preparing a completely new unit would give Virginia greater freedom. When Virginia shared her ideas for the unit, Marjorie added a few suggestions and concluded, "I can't wait to see how the students respond to your creative ideas."

During Virginia's lesson, one of Marjorie's students said, "Wow, look, Ms. Felstone is taking notes, too."

"Yes," Marjorie explained, "I like Ms. Nugent's ideas, and I would like to use some of them next semester."

By openly taking notes, Marjorie validated Virginia as a teacher and indicated her own willingness to reverse roles and again become a learner. Without jealousy or hesitation, she gracefully conceded the power in the classroom to her student teacher, demonstrating that learning is a lifelong process.

By thinking like a mentoring coach, you can set the tone for a successful relationship. Mentors often realize that since beginning teachers are usually recent university graduates, they may have technological expertise, may know innovative strategies, or be aware of effective multicultural resources. As your mentoring relationship progresses, you may rediscover the joy of learning from the beginning teacher.

These three steps—encouraging questioning, recognizing territoriality, and being a continuing learner—will enable you to become a more effective mentor and transform your mentoring relationship into a reciprocal partnership.

✖ · Becoming a Reflective Dialogue Coach · ✖

To make the mentoring relationship an enriching experience for the beginning teacher, schedule regular time for thoughtful conversation. During these conversations, establish a collegial relationship by conferring, questioning, mirroring, and reflecting.

Mentoring Through Conferring

Effective mentoring requires time. Giving the beginning teacher a quick solution to a problem takes an exchange of only a few sentences; coaching the beginning teacher into a deeper understanding of what is happening in the classroom demands longer, more structured sessions together. Helping beginning teachers to discover a solution for themselves builds self-confidence.

Raymond: *I'm having trouble getting kids to do their daily assignments in algebra class. What do you think I should do?*

Gayle: *What have you tried?*

Raymond: *I've tried lowering their grades and giving them detention, but that doesn't seem to help. One time I even doubled their homework as a punishment.*

Gayle: *Did that help?*

Raymond: *No, the same kids didn't do their homework.*

Gayle: *Why do you think they're not doing their work?*

Raymond: *I have no idea. I suppose I could ask them.*

Gayle: *Do you think they understand the homework?*

Raymond: *Well, I think so. Sometimes, though, my explanation of a new math lesson lasts until the bell rings. Then we don't have time for in-class work. Maybe some of them don't understand the homework problems.*

Gayle: *Do you think it's easier for them to finish homework at home if they can start it in class and get help on what they don't understand?*

Raymond: *Probably.*

Gayle: *What do you think you might try?*

Raymond: *Tomorrow I think I'll ask them to write down anonymously why they do or don't do their algebra homework. Then I could give them work time in class, and I could walk around the room and check their first two answers and see if they understand what we're doing.*

Gayle: *Well, you've analyzed the problem and thought of a few possible solutions. I'll be eager to hear what you discover.*

Gayle could have given Raymond an easy answer: "What usually works for me is . . ." Instead, she coached him through the situation, encouraging him to talk to her as he analyzed the reasons for the homework problem and considered possible solutions. She showed Raymond another way to approach the situation—maybe it isn't an "attitude"; maybe the students simply don't understand the material and are reluctant to ask questions. Next time, he will know that an "effect" can have a number of possible causes and attend more closely to his students' needs.

Gayle and Raymond found that talking after school for a few minutes several times a week was a good way to stay in touch. In the same way, you and your beginning teacher can decide on an effective way to communicate, such as chats or notes. Some mentors like the informality of talking together while walking to the lunchroom or faculty lounge; others prefer a formal meeting time. Work out a format and schedule that best accommodates your teaching and communication styles.

If your school day does not allow enough time for in-depth discussions with your beginning teacher, consider sharing a dialogue journal. This could be as simple as posing and replying to a list of questions in writing, or it could involve a longer statement of your teaching philosophy, style, and methods. If you talk with a student about disrespectful behavior in class, for example, you might also discuss the incident with the beginning teacher, explaining your approach and your reasons for it. Here, Rhonda explains to Sheri, a beginning teacher, how she worked through a troublesome situation:

Rhonda rubbed her forehead in frustration. "Sheri, today I had to talk to a student about cheating."

Sheri leaned forward. "What did you do? Did you tear up the paper?"

Rhonda shook her head. "That's what I used to do. Then I realized that it didn't solve anything. Instead, I asked the boy why he had cheated."

"What did he say?"

"He told me that he didn't understand the chapter, so it was easier to look at another student's paper."

"Are you going to fail him?"

"What I learned is that I failed. He didn't understand some of the basic economics principles covered in the chapter. When I looked at the other papers, I realized that many of the other students didn't understand them either."

"Are lots of students going to fail?"

"No, that wouldn't be fair. They need to understand these basics before we move on. I'm going to have to reteach one section of the chapter."

"Aren't you concerned about getting through the textbook?"

Rhonda smiled. "What I'm concerned about is that they haven't been learning. To me, learning is more important than covering the material."

"OK, so will you teach it the same way?"

"I think I might try something different. Tonight I'm going to think about how these economic principles apply to their teenage lives so I can try to connect with them tomorrow." Rhonda paused a few moments and then added, "Maybe I'll also ask them to do a three-minute quick write at the end of the period telling me what they've learned. Then I can see if they understand the principles now instead of waiting until the test."

Curious, Sheri asked, "Then you'll give the test?"

"I might even change the test. Maybe I'll give students time in class to write their own business scenario, applying the economic terms. That will eliminate any chance of cheating, and besides, I'll be better able to assess whether they've really learned them."

"That almost sounds fun."

"You're right," Rhonda agreed. "Maybe we could act out the scenarios. After they've seen different examples, they're more likely to get the big picture. Besides," she added, "that will reinforce what they have learned." She smiled reassuringly at Sheri. "Talking to you makes me more excited about it. I can't wait to try it."

During their conference, Rhonda modeled how she thought through a problem and arrived at viable strategies to resolve it. By admitting that even an experienced teacher can fail, Rhonda may have opened the door for Sheri to be more forthcoming about her own problems. The situation also allowed Rhonda to illustrate that education encompasses both teacher and student learning.

Down the hall from Rhonda and Sheri, Jon and Phyllis found that Jon's after-school basketball practices made it difficult to schedule adequate time for talking. At first they decided to meet once every week and later, once every two weeks. During the week, they both used sticky notes to jot down single comments or questions during class. Then they chose one comment and one question to exchange with each other on the day before their conference. That evening, each considered the other's question in order to come to their meeting with questions or examples. For many mentors and beginning teachers, this technique helps to focus attention on specific issues of concern.

Your methods of response and types of feedback depend on your mutual needs or individual preferences. Some mentors may prefer direct conversations rather than written journal exchanges, but written feedback from a mentor can be helpful to the beginning teacher in referring back to the exchange. Novices often recall only your constructive criticism and forget your positive statements. Written praise may serve as a reminder and an esteem-builder.

Whatever your conference style or your timetable, make the conferences work for you and your beginning teacher. Try various techniques to see which seem most productive.

Mentoring Through Questioning

Encouraging the beginning teacher to ask questions, both procedural and theoretical, can be an important part of mentoring. An inexperienced teacher may feel uncomfortable asking questions that could be interpreted as signs of ignorance or construed as criticism. Convey your interest with comments like these:

- What do you consider the most effective teaching moment in your class today? Why? How did you achieve it? What signaled you that students were learning?

- I'm eager to hear any questions you might have. What would you like to ask?

Asking open-ended questions offers the beginning teacher and you a way to identify and discuss issues that might not occur to you on your own. The following questions are useful in initiating mentoring discussions:

1. What was one of your successes as a teacher during the past week?

2. What do you see as your teaching strengths? What are the best things you have to offer kids?

3. How are you attempting to create a warm, friendly learning environment in your classroom? How are you forming a learning community?

4. On a scale of 1 to 10, how would you rate this day (week)? Why?

5. During what part of today did you feel that "real" teaching and learning was going on in your classroom?

6. How do you know when students are learning?

7. Which accomplishments as a teacher are you most proud of?

8. What is your greatest concern at this time?

9. What seems to be going well in your classroom management? What problems do you see?

10. Have you made any changes in your teaching strategies recently? What new techniques have you tried?

11. What factors make some of your lessons flow better than others?

12. If you could get beyond the day-to-day planning, what areas would you like to work on?

13. What successes have you experienced in working with parents? How could you expand your interaction with them?

14. Which aspects of teaching make you feel least comfortable?

15. Do you have any questions you would like to ask me?

Formulating and asking questions helps beginning teachers develop critical thinking skills to analyze their own teaching.

New teachers who have difficulty in listing their teaching strengths can take a strengths-finder test or, better yet, both mentor and mentee can take the online test and discuss its revelations (http://sf2.strengthsfinder.com/; Liesveld and Miller 2005).

Because of their inexperience, beginning teachers may not see or respond to situations like veteran teachers. Delores Westerman's (1991) research identified four major differences between expert and novice decision making. First, experienced teachers integrated present learning with past and future learning and drew connections to other disciplines. Beginning teachers, however, tended to rely on grade-level curriculum objectives and had more difficulty in making cross-disciplinary connections, most likely because they were unfamiliar with the curriculum at other grade levels.

Second, the study noted a difference in classroom management strategies. To motivate students and engage their attention, experienced teachers used a whole repertoire of techniques combining voice, gestures, and their reading of students' body language. Novice teachers, on the other hand, ignored off-task behavior until it escalated and then interrupted the lesson with a verbal reprimand or a punishment such as detention. In essence, veteran teachers tended to use proactive strategies to prevent management problems while beginning teachers waited for the problem to arise and then used reactive techniques.

Third, experienced teachers were more likely to see the "big picture." In planning lessons, they employed different thinking strategies—visualizing the lesson, predicting problems, and preparing alternatives. Novice teachers, on the other hand, had a "maybe it will work-maybe it won't" attitude. They waited for problems to arise instead of trying to anticipate how the activities they planned would play out in the classroom.

Fourth, experienced teachers evaluated their lessons according to their students' needs and growth in understanding, whereas novice teachers judged their lessons according to students' reactions and their achievement of the original objective. Once again, the veteran teachers were more tuned in to what their students needed and how they could meet those needs.

As these four points indicate, veteran teachers may use approaches to teaching that are more proactive, integrated, and perceptive than those employed by beginning teachers who, in struggling to survive, may not be experienced in the "best teaching practices" (Zemelman, Daniels, and Hyde 1998). Some of your mentoring sessions should concentrate on these areas: how to ascertain students' prior knowledge and make connections to their future learning, use proactive management strategies, visualize lessons and predict problems, create alternative plans, determine what students need, and judge whether learning has occurred. Here Larry "walks" Jacob, a beginning teacher, through preparations for a field trip.

Larry: *Next Friday, a week from today, you'll be taking the sixth graders to see the state capitol and the state historical building. What preparations have you made?*

Jacob: *We have a bus, four parent chaperones, and permission slips signed by parents or guardians. Jessica took care of the historical building arrangements, and I have talked to Betsy, our tour guide at the capitol building.*

Larry: *That's great. How are you planning to prepare your social studies classes for this trip?*

Jacob: *Well, actually I was planning to use next week to finish a unit on the Civil War, so I wasn't planning to do anything.*

Larry: *Maybe this is a teachable moment. Let's think about how you can make this trip relevant to students. How could you discover what students already know about the capitol building?*

Jacob: *I suppose I could ask them who had already toured the capitol and what they remembered.*

Larry: *That sounds good.*

Jacob: *But when am I going to finish the Civil War unit?*

Larry: *It will be OK to do that next week. How can you connect this field trip to what they're learning now about the Civil War?*

Jacob: *Hmm, well, I'd like to see the capitol before the trip. I'm hoping to go there this weekend, but since it's a two-and-a-half-hour drive, if something comes up and I can't go, I may have to rely on Betsy, the tour guide. If I can't get there, I could ask her to send me a layout of the building. Jessica is taking care of the historical building arrangements, and she has made this neat sheet of facts for the kids. I think she's been taking students there for the last ten years, so [chuckling] she probably knows about as much as the tour guides. I'll ask her what ideas she has to connect the trip to the Civil War unit. Maybe she could tell me which artifacts pertain to the Civil War so I could prepare the students a little before we go.*

Larry: *Great idea. You would then be integrating the field trip into the curriculum. What else could you do to prepare the students?*

Jacob: *Well, I guess we could review other aspects of state history, and I could check with their previous teachers to find out what the students already know.*

Larry: *That sounds helpful. Now, how are you going to prevent management problems?*

Jacob: *I don't know. I guess I wasn't expecting any problems on the field trip. What do you think will happen?*

Larry: *Well, how can you prevent students at the back of the bus from throwing paper or mooning drivers on the road?*

Jacob: *You've got to be kidding! Would sixth graders do that?*

Larry: *I hope not, but it helps to think through possible problems in advance.*

Jacob: *Gee, maybe the teachers could sit at different places in the bus so the kids would be less likely to goof off.*

Larry: *OK, and what directions will you give students before they get off the bus?*

Jacob: *I can see that I need to do a lot more thinking about this. Let me think about it this weekend, and we can talk again on Monday. I didn't know there was so much to consider.*

Larry's active planning and anticipation of potential problems showed Jacob that the field trip involved much more than simply moving sixth graders to and from the state capitol. He hadn't considered how it could tie into their history unit, and he certainly hadn't prepared for behavioral problems. Larry might also find it necessary to augment Jacob's knowledge of the tour's highlights so Jacob can prepare the students for what they will see and why it is significant.

In Monday's conversation, Larry might find other ways to help Jacob see the "big picture." For instance, he might ask, "What aspects of the capitol and historical building tour do you think will most fascinate sixth graders?" to help Jacob visualize the trip through sixth-grade eyes. Larry might also ask, "After the trip, how will you know if this has been a good educational experience?" to help Jacob think about how to recognize when students' attention is engaged and they are learning.

Jacob has the disadvantage of inexperience: he does not fully realize what could happen—and what should happen—on the field trip. But some beginning teachers operate by instinct, by what "feels right." Already, they can be recognized as "natural teachers." To help these new teachers connect their instincts to their natural judgment, mentors can demonstrate ways of evaluating sudden inspirations. Here, Martha is encouraging Jared, her student teacher, to think about the "why" behind his teaching strategies:

Martha: *I liked the partner groups you used today with the seventh graders.*

Jared: *Thanks. I thought they worked OK, too.*

Martha: *You didn't mention this activity earlier, during our planning period. Was this something you planned or a spur-of-the-moment idea?*

Jared: *I didn't plan to do it. It just seemed right.*

Martha: *What caused you to change the lesson? I'm curious.*

Jared: *Well, we were just wheeling along, and I thought I was doing an awfully good job, and then I looked at them, and they had not one clue about what was going on. I thought, "They don't get it. Wait. What can I change here?" So I asked them to work with a partner and write down what they understood and what they were still confused about.*

Martha: *Why do you think it worked?*

Jared: *I had been the one doing all the talking, and their only job was to listen. I guess sharing with a partner made them become actively involved.*

Martha: *What skills did students get to use in the partner groups?*

Jared: *Well, instead of just listening to me, they had to summarize the lesson in their own words, listen to a classmate, and compose their questions together. I didn't realize it then, but I guess they had to use speaking, listening, and writing. They were also using both auditory and visual senses.*

Martha: *That's great. What messages do you think this sends to the students?*

Jared: *Well, I suppose it told them that I really wanted them to learn this, and that it was OK to ask questions. Wow, I didn't realize that I had done all that until just now in talking about it with you. That's pretty cool.*

Through Martha's astute questioning, Jared proceeded to think through the elements of active involvement, using multiple senses, and respect for students that are part of the theoretical basis of his practice. By recognizing "why it worked" and seeing beyond the surface of his teaching strategies, Jared gave an intellectual structure to his natural instincts. The mentoring conversation prompted Jared to think reflectively, a skill he can now begin to pursue independently. His sudden shift in class activities was not a whim but an outgrowth of sound educational theory.

In addition to asking effective questions, mentors can help beginning teachers to formulate questions of their own. As the semester progresses, the beginning teacher's comments and questions should move from being self-centered to being more student-centered. Beginning teachers typically ask, "How am I doing?" As they realize the need to be sensitive to students' learning—or noncomprehension—they will start to ask, "How well are the students learning?" When beginning teachers shift from thinking about "me" to thinking about "them," they have made an important developmental step. Understanding that true education is not teaching but learning can be a monumental breakthrough. A beginning teacher may do a phenomenal job lecturing to a class, doing so-called teaching, but if the students cannot understand and apply the concepts, then the teaching has not been effective.

When beginning teachers watch a videotape of themselves teaching, they usually self-consciously notice their own appearance, speech patterns, and gestures. While these factors may be important, the "real" learning from the videotape may be in observing students' behavior. Through questioning, mentors can direct beginning teachers' attention to whether students are attentive, sleepy, or bored. A mentor might say, "What do you see students saying and doing that shows they have learned? Let's replay the tape and look for evidence of learning as we watch your lesson again."

Mentors can assist beginning teachers in making this professional leap from teaching to learning by first introducing the concept. Rick, a social studies teacher, told his student teacher, "When you start seeing student learning as your goal, then we'll really celebrate." Second, mentors can focus mentoring conversations on the question of how you know when students are learning. An extended discussion of this topic can direct beginning teachers to a focal point for each class period. Third, when beginning teachers do begin to express their thinking in terms of student learning, mentors can point out to them that this noticeable transformation is truly thinking "like a teacher." Then both, as Rick says, can "celebrate." This shift in perspective is an indication of the effectiveness of your mentoring.

Mentoring Through Mirroring

"Mirroring" is another effective mentoring strategy. You might

- Repeat an important point by the beginning teacher: "You said that student choice is important. How do you plan to use student choice?"

- Restate a comment: "I hear you saying that you think the students needed to be more actively involved today."

- Summarize dialogue and actions: "You said that you were upset with Simon because of his immature behavior, but by talking through the situation with him you indicated that you were more concerned about his future behavior."

During a mentoring conference, you might mirror a classroom interaction between a beginning teacher and a student by describing it and then reinforcing the teacher's words: "I heard you tell Sally that her assignment was late and that the grade would be lowered. Then you said that you knew she usually was a responsible person and that you were sure her future assignments would be in on time. I liked your firmness about the present action and your positive view of her future behavior."

In the following example, Darrell, a history teacher, employs a variety of mirroring strategies with Chad, a beginning teacher:

Chad: *I'd like to help the fifth graders really understand the transcontinental railroad. In college we were always taught to use hands-on stuff, so I thought maybe the students could build their own railroad.*

Darrell: *You're saying you want students to be actively involved? A student-centered approach?*

Chad: *Uh-huh.*

Darrell: *So what ideas do you have?*

Chad: *Well, first I thought maybe we could involve the entire building and have each classroom choose a name, like a town. They could make a mailbox outside their room and write letters to other classes. Some of my students could be Pony Express riders and deliver the mail.*

Darrell: *I hear you saying that you want this to be an all-school project. How are you going to get the cooperation of all of the teachers?*

Chad: *I hadn't really thought about it [pauses and thinks]. But I remember how the principal said he wanted us to do more interdisciplinary projects this year.*

Darrell: *We'll come back to how you're going to get support. What are your other ideas?*

Chad: *Then I want to show how the railroad took over for the Pony Express. I thought about having the students build a railroad along the edge of the hallway from one end of the building through the halls to the other end.*

Darrell: *So this will be another all-school project? What are the benefits?*

Chad: *That way every student in every grade—and everyone who visits the school—will see the railroad and might ask about it. It would be visual, you know. Each day two students from each railroad team could leave class for five minutes to lay down some tracks at each end. We could have the tracks meet in the gym, and then we could have an all-school assembly to lay the golden spike. It would make history come alive for them.*

Darrell: *I hear you saying that you want to make your class into a Pony Express team and then two railroad teams. Then you're also going to encourage the entire school to be involved in a Pony Express, letter writing, transcontinental railroad, and an all-school assembly.*

Chad: *It sounds like a lot when you restate it like that. But I still think I can do it.*

Darrell: *How would you convince the faculty to take on this project?*

Chad: *Well, I'd talk about how it would involve all the students.*

Darrell: *OK, active student involvement, that's good.*

Chad: *The students could see the railroad going up before their eyes. I guess my methods teacher would call that "visual reinforcement."*

Darrell: *[laughs] Great! Any others?*

Chad: *It would bring all of our subject areas together.*

Darrell: *Yes, interdisciplinary teamwork—that's a good one.*

Chad: *I guess I should write those ideas down so I could convince the faculty and administration.*

Darrell: *So where do you go from here?*

Chad: *Gosh, when you say it like that, it sounds as if maybe I'd better get it all down on paper and plan it out. Then I can go talk to the principal, and if he goes for it, maybe he'll give me time to talk at a staff meeting. I could send letters home and…*

Darrell: *You said that you plan to write it all out. Has that helped you before?*

Chad: *[chuckling] If I've learned anything, it's that my strength is creativity, but my weakness is planning. I don't dare fly by the seat of my pants. I'm going to write it all down first. Then I'll let you see it.*

During their conference, Chad shared his creative ideas with Darrell, but he really hadn't thought them through. Darrell used mirroring combined with questioning to show Chad where he was in his planning and where he still needed to go. By the end, Darrell had helped Chad devise a more realistic plan for thinking about his project and determining the best way to proceed. Through mirroring, beginning teachers like Chad rehear their words and revisit their actions so they can center their classroom activities on student learning.

Mentoring Through Modeling Reflection

Modeling reflective thought is another way of mentoring. Just as you demonstrate your leadership role through interactions with students, communicating with parents, and conversations with colleagues, you can model thinking about teaching. Reflective thinking usually occurs silently, in your mind, but you can also think aloud. Nancie Atwell (1998) refers to this technique as "taking off the top of your head." She models what she is thinking as she writes. Sometimes, for example, she stands at the overhead projector and talks aloud while writing various ideas for an opening sentence. In this way, students observe how a writer thinks and see that good sentences may not appear magically but result from systematic thought.

It might be helpful to show the beginning teacher how you think when you are planning. To "take off the top of your head," you might list the ideas you considered in teaching an area such as percentages for a math lesson and explain why you abandoned some and kept others. ("We're covering percentages… shall we start with fractions, or shall we look at the members of the class as equaling 100 percent and divide into groups to figure percentages of the whole?…") In addition to showing how you think as you plan, you can illustrate how you evaluated and used what happened in the classroom.

Terrance told Shane, his student teacher, "I like the fact that the students actively participated in the review game I made up, but I wonder whether they were really thinking about their responses or just watching to see if their team was winning. It's fine that they enjoyed it, but what I really want is for all of them to be thinking the whole time." By speaking his thoughts aloud, Terrance demonstrated some of the ways an effective teacher thinks about and questions his teaching practices and his students' learning. The beginning teacher can see that teaching is an ongoing process, one of planning, doing, questioning, and thinking.

By revealing your "thinking about your own thinking," you demonstrate how to think like a teacher. Beginning teachers often know how to "act" like a teacher, but they don't always understand the internal processes necessary to "be" a teacher, to think in an ongoing way about student learning. By talking about the idea that materialized while you were in the shower, the concerns that kept nagging at you during your evening walk, or the creative strategy that occurred to you as you were driving home from school, you model the continuous nature of teacher-thinking, which doesn't stop when you walk out the school door.

Michael, a middle school art teacher, observed his mentor, George, a social studies teacher, and his interdisciplinary team members (who were also his team mentors) discussing a Native American unit planned for the following semester:

> George looked around the group. "Last week," he reminded them, "we decided that we would all think about ideas for this unit. As I thought about this over the last few days, I decided a great idea would be to go on a field trip to a Native American museum. Then I realized that, with our tight school budget, we probably don't have the money. We also don't have the money for mileage and a speaking fee for a guest speaker."
>
> Michael watched as his team members sadly nodded. George continued, "We could use some documentary films, but that seems to be what we always do. I've been thinking about this and rolling ideas around in my head. Then last night, when I saw my son playing video games, I wondered if we could create a virtual field trip."
>
> Suddenly the room seemed to come alive as the team members asked one question after another. George shrugged, saying, "Well, that's as far as I got with my

idea. I've noticed, though, that the students seem to lack research skills, so I wondered if there would be some way we could use research."

Francie, a language arts teacher, intervened, "I've been thinking about research, too. One part of me wants to have the students work together in groups, but another part of me wants to encourage the students to be individually responsible. Our team's mission statement emphasizes both. I was thinking about this while I was getting dressed this morning, and I wondered whether we could have students grouped by Native American tribes, and each student could do individual research on one aspect of the tribe and compose a written paper. Then the group could work together on a presentation."

Vicki, a science teacher, linked the two ideas: "Maybe we could film their presentations. Showing the videotapes could be the virtual field trip."

At this point, the math teacher, Maria, entered the discussion. "Those are good ideas," she said, "but I've been thinking about it from a different angle. I wonder whether we want to show Native Americans of the past or today—or maybe both. I've also been thinking about how to work math into this project. I'll think about it some more and let you now."

As Maria talked, Michael mused about how art could be interwoven into the project. Murals? Dioramas? Pottery? In listening to his team members, he realized that he would need to think about the unit at some length, set aside unfeasible ideas, determine the students' information and procedural needs, and connect the unit to the team's and school's standards. Before he became a teacher, Michael thought every idea came from a textbook; now he recognized the depth of teacher-thinking devoted to each unit. He looked forward to the next team meeting to see how the group would continue to plan and the creative ideas he might share.

By observing his interdisciplinary team, Michael noted that team members thought about their teaching not only during planning sessions but also well beyond the school day. This kind of insight lifts teaching to a higher level for beginners as they learn how to truly "be" teachers. The mentor who also lets the beginning teacher observe him or her keeping up with the field—by reading professional journals and books, sharing ideas and information with colleagues, and participating in professional associations—further enlarges the context of the educational enterprise (see Chapter 12).

✎ · Summary · ✎

Conferring, questioning, mirroring, and reflecting all promote the beginning teacher's professional growth. These strategies offer ways to coach beginning teachers to "think like a teacher." By using these techniques, mentors help new teachers see beyond the superficial "fun times" of a field trip to the long-range educational benefits that accompany active student engagement. These mentoring strategies allow beginning teachers to get the whole picture. All take time, but the benefits to both mentor and new teacher are substantial: many enjoy a collegial relationship not only during the mentoring period but also for many years to come.

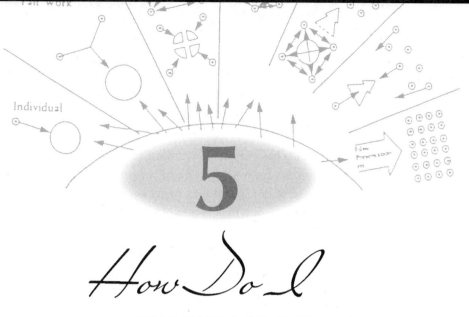

5

How Do I

ENCOURAGE REFLECTION?

Active, persistent, and careful consideration of any belief or supposed form of knowledge in light of the grounds which support it, and the further conclusions to which it tends, constitutes reflective thought.

—John Dewey, *How We Think*

Experienced teachers are familiar with the rhythms of the school day: the quick pace, the multiple interruptions, the moments of crisis. Their substantial experience informs their decisions about teaching and their sense of how well their students are learning. To the untrained eye, these teachers make teaching look effortless, even easy. They expertly weave activities together in an intricately patterned tapestry that seems to take shape by itself.

Beginning teachers have also had extensive experience of school. We often forget that as students, they observed thousands of hours of teaching and learned much about school cultures and structures—the beginning and end of school days and years, school functions, dances, sporting events, and graduations. Most have subsequently spent a year or more studying schools and teaching in university methods courses.

Unlike veteran teachers, however, beginning teachers have had scant experience working as the sole responsible professional in a classroom and limited knowledge of the demands placed on teachers: they haven't called parents, taken attendance, or kept a grade book. They haven't participated in faculty meetings, refereed classroom arguments, negotiated or designed curriculum, or planned daily instruction. After a month in her fourth-grade classroom, Sulema, a first-year teacher, felt a little desperate: "I wasn't ready for the demands," she told her mentor, Hillary. "I mean, the students are great, but the responsibility for keeping everything in order is, well, sometimes it's overwhelming."

Beginning teachers like Sulema have much to contribute to the lives of their students. They bring an abundance of energy and a fresh perspective to teaching. But as the challenges and demands increase over the course of the school year, many beginning teachers find that they need strategies to help them reflect on and make sense of what happens in their classroom.

✑ · Why Reflection? · ✑

Reflection is essential to a fully lived professional life. Among teachers, the finest are those who consider their progress in the classroom, who ponder effective teaching strategies and devise creative classroom activities, who practice reflection to set personal and professional goals, who think on their feet as they teach. These educators are the exemplars and leaders and mentors in our schools.

Unlike their seasoned mentors, beginning teachers such as Sulema often feel barely a day or an hour ahead in their lesson planning. Although they have completed student teaching or an extended practicum, these new teachers simply aren't used to the complexities of teaching—which often explains why the initial weeks in the classroom seem overwhelming. As newcomers to the profession, they often spend all their free time preparing for the next day's teaching. Activities and a focused plan ensure that there will at least be classroom activity.

Systematic reflection, however, can significantly enrich a novice teacher's understanding. Especially at the beginning of their careers, new teachers need to step back and look at their classroom practices. Reflection

- Helps beginning teachers organize their thoughts and make sense of classroom events.

- Leads to professional forms of inquiry and goal setting.

- Promotes a model of learning that views teaching as an ongoing process of knowledge building.

- Promotes conversation and collaboration with mentors.

Mentoring offers experienced teachers an important opportunity to cultivate in their younger colleagues a critical disposition that will guide their reflective practices. New teachers feel under pressure to plan and organize classroom instruction even as they are managing each day's emotional and cognitive challenges. For those who, like Sarah, have not completed a student teaching experience and who are starting teaching with a temporary credential, the challenges may be more substantial. In her journal, which she shared with Candice, her mentor, she wrote,

> *This week I had two teachers' meetings after school, then I planned for the unit I'm team teaching . . . One night this week I was up until 2:00 in the morning completing report cards . . . I also go to State and take classes at night to complete my credential . . . I'm all for reflecting in my journal, but what I want to know is, no offense, but am I wasting my time writing to you in this journal?*

Sarah's question about "wasting" time is legitimate: she is busy. But she needs to know that writing in her journal is one way to develop her knowledge and her skills. This is where Candice, her mentor, can be helpful. Mentors can talk with beginning teachers about why reserving time from a busy professional life to consider and reconsider their teaching can enhance their classroom practice. But it is equally important that mentors also support beginning teachers in their attempts to be reflective.

Reflection as a Sense-Making Process

Reflection is a critical function of successful teaching and learning, whatever an individual's experience or level of education. Reflection can be defined as an analytical process of data-gathering and sense-making through which teachers deepen their understanding of teaching and learning. Nearly a hundred years ago, the philosopher John Dewey (1910) wrote about the importance of reflective thinking. He characterized it as a sense-making process arising from a "felt need," usually in the form of an open-ended question about pedagogy or student learning. The reflective process continued with an active investigation directed toward bringing to light further facts to corroborate or to nullify the suggested belief (9). In the classroom, teasing apart a perplexing situation or problem and seeking a solution or an explanation guides and propels reflective inquiry.

As a mentor working with a beginning teacher, you can be an important catalyst for reflection. You are, after all, a presence in the new teacher's life whose suggestions carry influence; your actions and reactions will shape your colleague's behavior and perspective. An excellent way to promote reflection is to demonstrate your own reflective processes and actions and their benefits, possibly by having the beginning teacher observe you or other team mentors periodically throughout the school year. School districts that sponsor mentoring programs often provide release time for beginning colleagues to observe their mentors and other master teachers in action.

Besides demonstrating reflective behavior and activities, you can also promote reflection in beginning teachers by documenting their teaching performance in the classroom. Your well-trained eyes watching and keeping track of classroom action can gather invaluable information. Having a way to describe reflective action to the beginning teacher will also help you to promote reflective thinking.

Types of Reflection

Donald Schön's (1983) *The Reflective Practitioner: How Professionals Think in Action* describes reflection as a necessary means for engaging in professional activity. By studying professionals and their apprentices as they solved "design problems," he developed categories of reflective thinking, two of which we discuss below.

Reflection-on-Action. Reflection-on-action involves a systematic analysis of professional activity or performance after a task is completed.

Ronaldo, a first-year language arts teacher working in a diverse, urban school, began the year planning and constructing all his lessons from scratch for his classes of more than thirty-five students. After a few weeks, however, he became disenchanted with his students' unacceptable behavior and low productivity. He articulated a "felt need" and began to talk with several of his colleagues about his teaching. Sensing a need to reconsider his teaching strategies, Ronaldo turned to his mentor, David, for assistance.

David scheduled time with Ronaldo to discuss the perceived "problem" at length. After listening to him carefully and discovering that he was a prolific writer, David recommended that he try to make sense of his students' behavior by writing as a way of thinking about it. Ronaldo began, and a week later he wrote in his journal:

During the first four weeks of instruction, I made the classic mistake of getting caught up in the curriculum. In an attempt to manage my 180 students, I dove head-

first into the pool of language arts, and to my surprise, my students dove right in after me. What I noticed was the blank stare in my students' eyes; they had absolutely no idea why they were swimming. It took me a while to realize that the reason I left school each day with a pounding headache was because I was doing way too much of the thinking. I was not only thinking for myself, but I was doing most of the thinking for my students. As a result of this epiphany, I now need to make independent thinking the primary issue inside our classroom.

This is an example of what Schön calls reflection-on-action: Ronaldo systematically documented and analyzed his teaching. His narrative helped him to work through what had happened in his classroom and to determine what he wanted to have happen. Eventually, Ronaldo's reflective writing produced an important insight about how to structure classroom activity. The solution included shifting responsibility for thinking to the students.

Reflection-in-Action. Unlike reflection that is planned, organized, and systematic in nature, reflection-in-action occurs in the midst of an activity and often results in the immediate reframing of a classroom situation or action. Reframing is the result of a sudden and unexpected flash of knowledge or understanding that enables a teacher to think and act differently and more productively. During one of her first lessons, Jasmine, a beginning elementary school teacher, issued oral directions to her students about completing a math problem in groups. As she scanned the room, however, she sensed their confusion. Some sat idly; others looked at each other blankly wondering how to proceed. She quickly reformulated the directions, wrote them on the chalkboard, and modeled the problem-solving process for all to see. Given clear directions and a sense of process, students began to work on their task. This is reflection-in-action: Jasmine relied on tacit knowledge to reframe the problem and then gave the directions in written and oral form so that students with different learning styles could understand the task.

⨯ · Activities That Promote Reflection · ⨯

The strategies that follow will enable you and the beginning teacher to collect information and document classroom procedures and to look at classroom culture and dynamics more carefully. They will also be useful in organizing this information so that you can offer structured feedback.

Over the years, we have tested and refined these activities and strategies, and we continue to use them with both beginning and veteran teachers. You can decide which work best in your own mentoring interactions.

Reflective Dialogues

A mentor teacher's most important tool in promoting reflection-on-action with the beginning teacher is dialogue. We rarely think of dialogue as a tool, yet talking about teaching can be a very effective way to deepen our understanding of classroom practice. Nothing is more important than setting aside time to talk with new colleagues about what is happening in their classrooms. Often a quick "How is it going?" is enough. They may be seeing their classrooms with fresh, enthusiastic eyes, but some of what they observe may confuse, mislead, or alarm them. Frequent conversations with a mentor will reassure them and give them the added benefit of a longer view that sees beyond current problems. Simply listening sometimes encourages a new colleague to talk her way through to a solution or to discover a different approach. Informal conversations like these can often do more to promote reflective thinking and inquiry than any amount of coursework.

Strategies to encourage reflective dialogue:

- Allocate time for one-on-one or group dialogue.
- Keep conversations confidential, since trust is essential.
- Listen and observe. Resist the urge to take over the conversation.
- Share recollections of your own early days in teaching, but be careful not to overwhelm your new colleague with too many "horror" stories.
- Use the information you gather during your class observations to generate talking points for substantive discussion. ("Are you dominating the class? How can you encourage students to take responsibility for classwide projects?")

Observing and Scripting Classroom Activity

Mentors may feel they need to observe a beginning teacher's classroom practice before they talk together about it, that simply asking, "How is it going?" will not engender a thoughtful exchange. Classroom observations are useful ways to launch a reflective dialogue. One way to document what you observe is to "script" a lesson or a series of lessons. "Scripting" involves describing and recording the student and teacher interactions, materials—pens, paper, texts, overheads, videotapes—and activities you observe in the classroom context. You can script by taking notes or by recording observations with the formats discussed in this chapter.

Documentation is often considered a task unique to administrators, who are responsible for formal evaluations of teaching performance, but even beginning teachers benefit from scripting, or recording, what their mentors or other colleagues say and do when they teach.

Since beginning teachers are usually nervous about their classroom performance, time spent observing exemplary, but not necessarily perfect, practice may ease their anxiety and provide subjects for thoughtful postlesson conversations—how, for example, veteran teachers organize their class and its activities, follow the curriculum, and manage student behavior.

Three months had passed since the beginning of the school year, yet Sarah, a beginning fourth-grade teacher, was nervous about Bobbie, her mentor, observing her teaching. Before visiting Sarah's classroom, Bobbie talked to Sarah about the observation and made it clear that the mentor's role was to support and guide—not to "evaluate." Bobbie wanted Sarah to know that the observations would lead to understanding, and, it was hoped, improved teaching.

Bobbie and Sarah met a day prior to observation to discuss the visitation. Bobbie and Sarah agreed that during the first few observations, Bobbie would focus on one aspect of teaching and that she would observe without scripting. So during the first classroom visit, Bobbie sat inconspicuously in the room and made mental notes, focusing on the opening of the class. She and Sarah worked on engaging openings to lessons that would get students quickly working and learning.

After the class, Bobbie talked briefly with Sarah about the observation and the opening of class. Bobbie understood that immediate feedback was essential to promoting thinking and learning, and she wanted to motivate Sarah to reflect on the class opening and to learn from it. Bobbie left suggesting that in their regularly scheduled meeting, they talk further about the class opening and discuss various scripting formats Bobbie would be using in the future.

After the initial observation, any of the following activities may prove helpful to the reflective exchanges of mentors and beginning teachers.

Noting General Impressions

One way to document classroom action is simply to note your general impressions. Locate an inconspicuous place in the classroom with a clear view of the students and the teacher and write down whatever comes to mind as you watch classroom activities unfold. You will probably end up with a page or two of notes or a list of thoughts about general classroom events.

Strategies to enhance this activity:

- Beforehand, explain to your new colleague what you will be writing down and why; do not keep your intent secret.

- Focus your observation on one or two events, questions, or issues.

- Do not overload your colleague with random observations about what he or she is doing "wrong"; balance your comments with positive statements about student and teacher performance.

- Talk with the beginning teacher shortly after the observation.

Chunking Classroom Activities

Managing time is often a challenge for beginning teachers. This exercise requires an observer to look with a "researcher's eyes": every five minutes, write down on a sheet of paper what the students and the teacher are doing (see Figure 5.1). We refer to this activity as "chunking" because it considers those classroom activities that occur during particular chunks of time; taken together these blocks make up the span of class time.

Teachers and students may, of course, devote more than five minutes to an activity. The purpose of chunking, however, isn't to encourage rapid-fire changes in classroom activities but to assist in developing a sense for sequence, pacing, and structure.

Strategies to enhance this activity:

- Wear a watch, or place one in view, so that you do not have to look at the wall clock, which may be located in an inconvenient place.

- On the right side of the paper, record observations that pertain to the chunk recorded on the left.

- Offer feedback shortly after the observation.

Analyzing Social Organization and Teaching Activities

Many beginning teachers need help in considering which organizational structure best promotes student learning in their classrooms. Sometimes, for example, a mini-lecture or direct instruction will clarify key concepts; at other times, sharing and learning in pairs or in small groups are more effective.

How a teacher organizes activities depends on several variables: the nature of the task or the material, the social and intellectual capabilities of the students, and the teacher's

Figure 5.1 Chunking Classroom Interactions

Time	Teacher/Student Activity	Observation
05		
10		
15		
20		
25		
30		
35		
40		
45		
50		
55		
60		
65		
70		
75		

personality. By analyzing the various structures, you can help the beginning teacher to consider these variables and to select the most effective.

Begin this exercise by documenting the types of organizational structures the teacher has used in a lesson (see Figure 5.2) and keep track of the amount of instructional time devoted to them.

Strategies to enhance this activity:

- Consider the content of the lesson and its relation to the organizational structure.

- Document the percentage of the lesson informed by the various organizational structures detailed in Figure 5.2.

- Present your information in the form of statistics rather than opinions; use the data to spark conversation, not to tender judgment.

Figure 5.2 Social Organization and Teacher Activity *(From Nunan 1990, 78)*

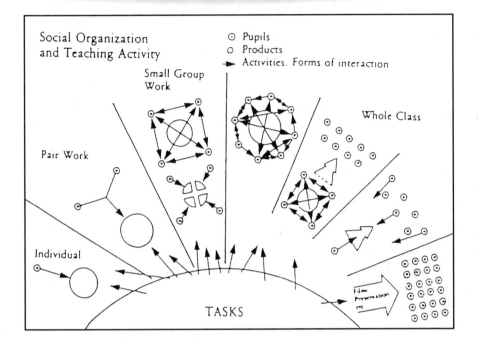

Charting Discussions and Questioning Techniques

Teachers often initiate a classroom discussion to promote students' sense of involvement and understanding. Research suggests that effective strategies for discussion can enhance student learning (Christenbury 2006; Marshall, Smagorinsky, and Smith 1995). Since discussion is such a powerful tool for learning, and much of what we do in classrooms involves talk, you might suggest to the beginning teacher that she think about how often she asks questions and what kind (yes/no, pseudo, vague, open-ended), and about the responses students offer. You and the teacher can both document these questions and responses using the coding system and format analysis developed by David Nunan (1990). This information offers a good starting point for conversation about questioning techniques that promote interaction, encourage critical thinking, and sustain intellectual development.

Strategies to enhance this activity:

- Using the adaptation of Nunan's coding system shown in Figure 5.3, note the types of teachers' questions and responses.

Figure 5.3 Analyzing Classroom Interactions/Questions *(Adapted from Nunan 1990, 82)*

Class _____ Date _____

Teacher _____

Interactions	Tallies	Total
1. Teacher asks a "pseudo"-question (a question to which she already knows the answer).		
2. Teacher asks an open-ended question (a question to which she does not know the answer).		
3. Teacher rephrases or recasts a question.		
4. Teacher probes response of learner.		
5. Teacher explains a vocabulary item.		
6. Teacher praises.		
7. Teacher answers her own question.		
8. Teacher explains a point relating to the content of the lesson.		
9. Teacher gives directions.		
10. Teacher criticizes.		
11. Learner asks a question.		
12. Learner responds/answers a question.		
13. Learner talks to another learner after a question.		
14. Period of silence or confusion.		
15. Other		

- Initially, code classroom discourse and formats without discussing the coding system or its purpose with the beginning teacher; you want the information you gather to be organic and uninfluenced by the observation tool.

- Encourage beginning teachers to visit other classrooms to observe and document class discussions. Play back videotapes of beginning teachers presenting a lesson and encourage them to use the coding system to analyze their style and habits in classroom discourse.

- Talk about the information gathered in the coding system shortly after the observation.

Mapping Classroom Landscapes

How a teacher arranges desks and learning space often reveals how she views and uses classroom areas. By gathering information about classroom layout ("mapping"), you can initiate a conversation about ways of arranging the classroom to increase student learning and interaction. In this exercise, the observer takes a visual inventory of the room's physical features. Where are students' desks? (Are they arranged in clusters? In a horseshoe? In rows? As chairs at tables?) Where is the teacher's desk? (At the front of the room? On the side?) Where does the teacher stand? Is there a class library, and if so, where is it located? Where do the bulletin boards hang, and how are they designed? (Is student work displayed? If so, how?) Mapping the classroom landscape like this focuses new teachers on the relationship between physical arrangements and student learning.

Strategies to enhance this activity:

- Use a full sheet of paper and draw the room, with desks; tables; chalk-, dry erase, or bulletin boards; and so forth. Capture it all.

- Sketch in the position of the desks or tables in the room; indicate where each student sits and the gender of each.

- Using this map as a reference, talk about the classroom environment and how its arrangement fosters—or inhibits—interaction and learning.

Charting Classroom Movement

Another excellent way to collect information is to chart the teacher's physical position in the classroom. Beginning teachers often mark out "power zones" in the front of the room and tend to avoid sections where particular groups of students sit. But as teachers, they need to be aware of their own movement and tendencies and of the activities in every part of the room. It is good practice for beginning teachers to circulate throughout the classroom and to monitor student activities.

Strategies to enhance this activity:

- Draw a map of the classroom that includes the location of students' desks or tables/chairs, the teacher's desk, and the front and back of the room.

- Section the room off into quarters and chart the behavior you see in each section, noting emerging patterns.

- Once you have drawn the map, trace the teacher's movement with a pencil, following it closely.

Writing to Reflect on Teaching

Journal. Writing in a journal is an effective way to reflect on classroom occurrences, events, conflicts, successes, and disappointments. By documenting and analyzing their experiences in a journal, beginning teachers learn to reflect-on-action. In their journal entries, they can capture and then critique what is working well and what is working poorly. Journals can also provide an important outlet for new teachers, who at the end of the day or the week need a place to unload and express their feelings.

Keeping a journal requires little in terms of materials. Any writing medium will do. Some like pen and notebook, others prefer computers. Regardless of the medium or the technology, the point of keeping a journal is to use writing to reflect on classroom practice and attempt to make sense of it. Here, mentor teachers can assist beginning teachers by writing themselves.

Although the act of writing down thoughts, ideas, and feelings is important, ideally the journal should lead to thoughtful conversations. Too often, educators require their students to keep journals but do not integrate this writing into purposeful classroom activities. The ideas remain on the margins instead of finding expression in new approaches and activities.

Ask questions that will guide the beginning teacher to writing, analysis, and critique: "How did you feel about today's lesson and how it unfolded?" A simple question may lead to a journal entry. Questions that focus on a specific issue or event, such as a mini-lesson or a small-group activity, might also encourage more thoughtful teaching.

When Bill began teaching, he assumed that every student in his tenth-grade class could read the stories and essays in the assigned textbook. Working in an inner-city school in Los Angeles, he quickly discovered, however, that many of his students couldn't decode or comprehend the textbook. Bill turned to his mentor, Estelle, a veteran teacher of eight years. She recommended that he reflect on what he was observing in a journal. Determined to do something about the situation, Bill began one journal entry with two guiding questions: "How many students in my classes can decode and comprehend the text?" and "Is the textbook too difficult for some of my students?" Bill wrote several pages on his observations about the challenges facing students reading below "grade level." Using what he had discovered from check tests and individual reading inventories, in another journal entry he concluded, "My students had difficulty decoding and comprehending even the simplest sentences in the text. What made matters worse was that the success of the unit depended on their ability to comprehend what they had read."

As Dewey (1910) noted, there must be a "felt need" to question before reflection or inquiry can happen. This does not necessarily mean that the questions have to be anchored in a classroom catastrophe. Beginning teachers often spotlight only unproductive activity: their inability to keep students engaged or on task; the lack of enough material or activities to fill the class period; the student who simply refuses to work or who is completely belligerent; or, as in Bill's case, students' inability to read. There is no denying that these are significant challenges, well worth consideration and reflection. Yet classroom teachers will always face challenges. The challenging aspects of teaching are usually balanced by successful practices or breakthroughs, and mentors should assist their new colleagues by focusing on what is working well. By looking at successful activities, beginning teachers can identify characteristics they can replicate in other areas of their classroom practice.

Strategies to enhance this activity:

- Use the journal as a place for dialogue. Read and respond to the new teacher's journal entries. You might consider trading off writing in the journal week by week or dividing each page down the middle and allocating one side to the new teacher's reactions and thoughts and the other to your comments and additional reactions.

- Encourage your new colleague to select one event or one episode and in the journal to develop it into a position statement, a point of departure for other classroom strategies or curriculum and assessment materials.

- Talk about the journal entries. Sometimes a simple ten- or fifteen-minute conversation can lead to wonderful insights and a more sophisticated understanding of students, of learning, and of the art of teaching.

Critical Incidents in One-Pagers. For those who think writing should be a tool for reflection but want an alternative to the journal, we suggest the "one-pager." A one-pager is a single page of writing whose purpose is to promote reflective thinking and dialogue. The limited amount of space forces the beginning teacher to focus his thinking about teaching by analyzing one or two observations or a critical incident.

To promote reflective analysis you might suggest dividing the one-pager into two parts. In the first part, the beginning teacher describes, in some detail, the event or happening; in the second, she can try to analyze the event and her thoughts and feelings about it (Tremmel 1993). Here, for example, Monica, a beginning sixth-grade teacher, reflects on a critical incident.

Part I (Description)

My principal gave each of us a packet of information for beginning teachers. Among the helpful hints was one which said, "Greet students by name at the door at the beginning of each class period." I decided to observe other teachers in my area and their classroom learning climates.

One teacher worked at her desk and did not speak to any student until after the second bell. Then she looked up and scowled . . . the students began working on the task, but they also talked to friends, sharpened pencils, passed notes, etc.

The second teacher stood at the door and greeted each student by name and involved the students in casual conversations about their interests or school activities. When I asked her about her rationale, she said, "I want students to know that I am glad to see them and that I am ready to work with them and not against them. You wouldn't invite someone to your home and ignore them until dinner was served, would you?"

Part II (Response to the Incident)

I never realized that the time between bells is an important time to interact with students and that it sets the tone for the class period. The second teacher's students seem to respect her because she respects them. I liked the analogy of welcoming the students into the classroom as being similar to greeting dinner guests . . . From this experience, I plan to greet and welcome my students into the classroom every day.

Strategies to enhance this activity:

- Respond to the one-pager with a one-pager of your own.
- Model and share your reflective processes in a one-pager.
- Talk about what you have both written.

Documenting and Analyzing with Video

Toni, a beginning teacher, stood at the front of the classroom in her "power zone" with her arms crossed. She rarely smiled or communicated her delight in teaching to her students. Yet after receiving feedback from Allison, her mentor teacher, she was surprised. She could not believe what she heard and took the reaction as a personal insult—until Allison asked her to videotape two of her lessons.

Toni took Allison's advice and videotaped several lessons in her ninth-grade language arts classes. Then she viewed the two lessons with her daughters; their honest responses provided Toni with important insights, as she explained to Allison shortly after she viewed the tapes: "I didn't want to believe what you were telling me. I mean I heard what you were saying, but I had no idea; I mean, I didn't think about what I was doing and how I looked. But then one of my daughters, who watched the tape at home, commented that I was boring. Can you imagine— boring! Hearing that from her and seeing it on the tape really hit home."

Capturing teaching on video gives beginning teachers like Toni a way of stepping back and gaining important distance. Often a mentor teacher notes a particular mannerism or procedure, but her comments fall on deaf ears. Any adverse reaction can seem like criticism, which puts a new teacher on the defensive. It could be that new teachers haven't developed the reflective capabilities that would let them see their teaching performance objectively. Videotapes provide distance and perspective. Newcomers may apply insights from videotapes immediately, as Toni did, or they can look back at earlier tapes to assess their improvement over time.

This is not to say that the video camera will not capture outstanding performances. It will! And these special moments of outstanding teaching should be highlighted and celebrated. New teachers view their classroom performance as pathologists: they hunt for what is wrong or broken, for activities that have failed or flopped. New teachers can learn from their failures, of course, but they can also learn from their successes.

Strategies to enhance this activity:

- Encourage videotaping of several classes two or three times during the semester or the academic year; a running record is important.

- Position the camera in different locations for each taping: in front, facing the students; in back, looking toward the front.

- If possible, arrange to have the video camera in the room a day or two before filming to give students time to get used to its presence.

- Check district or school policies about videotaping in the classroom.

⤞ · Reflection Promotes Professionalism · ⤞

The ability to draw back and reflect on your actions allows you to manage and make sense of the flood of images, feelings, and expectations you experience in the classroom. As a mentor, you can assist beginning teachers to deepen their understanding of classroom activity through thoughtful reflection and conversation. The information you gather during your classroom observations and follow-up dialogues with newcomers can help them set new goals for professional development.

To promote and encourage interaction and reflection, individual schools and school districts must allocate sufficient time for mentor programs so that veterans and beginners can work together. Conversation at a workshop or during lunch isn't enough. If they are to undertake a substantive review of their practice, beginning teachers need sustained periods of time during and after the school day to consider their teaching and their students' progress.

Allocating enough time to mentors is also essential. Mentors are generally busy classroom professionals whose schedules are as frenetic and full as the beginning teacher's. They should not have to "find time" during the day or after school to observe or talk with new colleagues. For mentors to be successful, they need ample time to work with beginning professionals in developing their teaching practice.

� · Summary · ✍

Reflective practitioners can continually improve their teaching performance by being more aware of ways to apply effective instructional strategies, engender positive student response, and set and attain personal and professional goals.

According to Schön (1983), reflection can take the form of reflection-on-action (reflecting on successes and concerns after the class period) and/or reflection-in-action (reflecting during teaching to make immediate changes to aid student learning).

Mentors can help beginning teachers by modeling reflection and by observing each other's classrooms. Various methods of documenting classroom activities include scripting teacher talk, noting general impressions, chunking activities, analyzing social organization and teaching activities, charting discussions and questioning techniques, mapping the classroom, charting teacher movement, journaling, and analyzing classroom videos. By documenting and analyzing classroom interactions, mentors and beginning teachers can reflect together on learning successes and problems.

Using reflection, both new and experienced teachers can examine *what* happened in the classroom as well as *why* it happened, thereby increasing teacher professionalism and maturity.

6

How Do I

HELP WITH CLASSROOM MANAGEMENT CHALLENGES?

"I just don't know what else to do with these sixth graders. I've tried being nice, I've counted seconds waiting for them to pay attention to me, and I've kept some of them after class. I even yelled today, and that got their attention for, oh, about thirty seconds. I'm so mad at myself; other people—you, for example—handle your classroom fine all the time. What's wrong with me? Why can't I control the class? I just can't face going back into that room."

Jane, a first-year teacher, confessed her frustration to her mentor, Carolyn, who smiled sympathetically. "You should have seen me my first year. If you had talked to me then, you would probably have been amazed at how much like you I sounded. There's no magic answer. I've picked up a few management skills over the years, but you need to realize that there is no one formula that works for everyone in every situation. There are some basic principles to live by, but you have to adapt them to each individual situation."

For many of us, classroom conflicts with students sap the joy out of our teaching lives. We entered the profession because we wanted to share our love for our subject, to teach students and enable them to do something with this knowledge, and to make a positive difference in their futures. The reality, however, is that we will not be able to accomplish these goals unless we can manage our classrooms.

Managing the classroom. What does that really mean to the beginning teacher? Those of us who have taught extensively understand that classroom management is simply the level of organization and order necessary for both students and teachers to accomplish their learning and instructional goals. This definition is intentionally flexible in order to allow for the great diversity of tasks and personalities, classrooms and contexts within which teachers and students find themselves. It also recognizes that teachers need different levels of calm or chaos to be comfortable—as do their students.

So why is a well-managed classroom often so hard for inexperienced teachers to achieve? We cannot dismiss the reality that we may have anywhere from twelve to thirty-five students, with distinct personalities, interests, and abilities, in our classrooms. This alone creates a huge challenge in lesson preparation, especially for the teacher who wants to acknowledge and accommodate various learning styles. Although Jane's frustration is a common one for student teachers and less-experienced teachers, seasoned professionals also have moments when their classroom management is less than perfect. In this section, we explore some reasons for management problems and suggest some principles that may help mentor teachers offer solutions to their less-experienced counterparts.

✄ · Problems and Challenges · ✄

Challenges Associated with Student Populations

Few school districts today can afford class sizes under twenty students. For the majority of teachers, classes typically have twenty-five to thirty-five students, and some as many as forty. Too often, classrooms lack adequate seating and space for the number of students they must accommodate, and teachers suffer from the problems associated with overly large class sizes. Indeed, teachers who have been successful with smaller classes often begin to encounter management difficulties when class size grows.

Another challenge for teachers is the successful inclusion of students with exceptional needs. While most of us applaud efforts to mainstream students, we must also acknowledge that the success of this initiative has sometimes complicated management choices. The majority of these students create no more problems than their classmates. However, there are occasions when inclusion students have not been adequately prepared to enter the mainstream classroom. Teachers find that they need to spend more time getting to know them and their unique strengths and needs. But teachers with a large number of inclusion students who may receive little support from resource teachers may find themselves spread so thin that problems ensue.

Teachers also face unmotivated or angry students who are impervious to their planning and good intentions. Many of these students are wrestling with overwhelming personal problems. Some have had negative experiences with other teachers or certain subject areas or feel that school does not offer them what they really need at this juncture in their lives. Naturally enough, students with this profile tend to present greater management challenges, even for sympathetic and concerned teachers.

Finally, some problems arise because students are young and emotionally volatile. Any classroom will include students who have disagreements, budding romantic relationships, or a desire to impress one another. Such interpersonal factors can be significant distractions, even for otherwise well-adjusted students. Although these interactions are clearly normal, they can create every bit as much disruption as more serious problems.

Teacher-Generated Problems

Most teachers graduate from excellent degree programs that equip them with more than enough content knowledge, but they may have had less direct instruction in management strategies. Universities are often overwhelmed by this task because management is unique to the individual teacher and the teaching situation; however, universities and educators must confront the situation more proactively.

Management problems also arise in the classroom because of poor—or no—preparation on the part of the teacher. We've all heard horror stories of teachers whose lesson plans read "Do adverbs, Warriner's, page 362." Such plans are unlikely to generate lessons that captivate every student's attention. A teacher who devotes little time to preparation may well deserve the management problems she gets.

On the other hand, some less-experienced teachers see themselves as the "stars" of the class. They plan their own role extensively but relegate students to the role of audience. Few students appreciate this role for long and are likely to assume the role of critic instead. In addition to planning concerns, newer teachers may give students few opportunities to contribute to class decision making. They may feel that they need to keep decision making in their own hands or students will take the class in directions with which the teachers are uncomfortable. In reality, however, students who sense no ownership in the course and no place for their ideas are more likely to create disturbances than those who are included in decision making.

All teachers hope their students will treat them respectfully, but respect must be reciprocal. Unfortunately, some teachers fail to offer the same respect to their students, sometimes because they feel they are the authority in the classroom, but also because they simply do not take the time to become thoroughly attuned to their students. Teachers may be unfamiliar with students' cultural backgrounds, academic levels, or interest in the subject, and this lack of audience awareness can also generate management problems.

Time management is closely related to classroom management. Most veteran teachers know that a class that begins promptly at the bell will be the class that holds its focus. However, inexperienced teachers often allow students to chat after the bell has rung while they take attendance, or talk to individual students about late homework, or organize papers for the beginning of class. Consequently, they may have difficulty redirecting students' attention to the task at hand.

It should go without saying—but doesn't—that setting rules and expectations for students early in the school year or semester is vital. Teachers are often responsible for these rules, and some collaborate with students to set expectations for the class. But Susan, a new middle school teacher, explained her rules and expectations quickly on the first day of class and failed to provide a poster or handout to reinforce these policies in her students' minds. Not surprisingly, when Phillip and Natalie turned in their project two days late without explanation, they insisted that they didn't realize they would be penalized. And when the two students' parents called to complain about the poor grades their children received on the project, Susan had no proof of her policy.

✒ · Principles of Management · ✒

Management Matters

> Linda sighed as she walked past Mark's old room. She would miss her former mentee; he had decided to resign after an especially difficult year with a group of rambunctious seventh graders. Although she had tried to support him by offering a variety of management suggestions, he had been unable or unwilling to adopt them.

Few people are drawn to teaching because it offers the opportunity to manage a classroom, but a great many people leave teaching because they can't or don't manage classrooms well. Despite our reluctance to encourage you to come across as excessively control oriented when you are discussing management with the teacher you mentor, there is no escaping the fact that ignoring management decisions can lead to a situation in which neither student nor teacher goals can be accomplished. If you have the opportunity to work with your beginning teacher before classes begin, it is wise to encourage her to think carefully about behavioral expectations and classroom routines.

Classroom Management Strategies Should Be Developed Before the School Year Begins

Although we have already mentioned it, we want to reinforce the idea that proactive planning is critical to the success of less-experienced teachers. Lin Su, a second-year fourth-grade teacher, remembered last year's management decisions vividly. She had decided not to give the "rule talk" to her fourth graders on the first day of class because she did not want to come across as the "heavy." The students responded to Lin Su's lack of direction by making every effort to determine how far she would let them go before reacting. By the end of the first week, Lin Su was contemplating early retirement even as the students embarked on a year of anarchy. She eventually restored order, but the process was lengthy and difficult. This year, she would do things differently.

If a teacher goes into the classroom and has to make management decisions on the spot, without the aid of a previously developed policy, problems are inevitable. A disruptive student who is reprimanded in front of classmates has an even greater incentive to contest teacher actions in order to "save face" if there is no management policy in place. Teachers who make their policies clear early in the semester have the flexibility to enforce or to modify those policies because the students already know the rules and what is expected of them.

Classroom Policies Should Be Simple to Explain and Easy to Enforce

Stan, a first-year teacher, has already decided that he will not be caught unprepared when management problems arise. Before the school year began, he spent hours developing policies for absences and tardiness, bathroom passes, late work, talking in class, respect for classroom furniture, respect for other students as well as the teacher, trips to the water fountain, and every other conceivable activity known to students. On the first day of class, he distributed a three-page management handout to every student and sent another copy home to parents. For each infraction, his management plan detailed the consequences for the first, second, and third occurrence. On his desk were individual infraction sheets that he intended to file by class period as well as the sheets he expected to use to keep track of how many points students lost for "one-day-late" work, "two-day-late" work, and so on.

Stan's is an example of the too-complex management plan. Prior preparation is admirable, but he has created a system so complicated that all his energies are likely to go into an unsuccessful attempt to maintain it. Stan instituted this management plan hoping that it would make his teaching life easier and convince his students that he was serious. However, the pressures of everyday school life and the inevitable exceptions that will arise will eventually make his professional life more difficult. In addition, he may inadvertently be leading his students and their parents to believe that he expects frequent misbehavior and that he lacks confidence in his own ability to work with them—and they may be right.

Although a carefully thought-out management plan is essential, it is also essential that the plan be practical. Stan's mentor should remind him that a system requiring extensive and detailed record keeping traps the teacher by its inflexibility and is prone to failure. Even if the teacher is capable of maintaining such a system, his or her time is better spent grading papers or homework, planning lessons, or conferring with students. (See Resources for Teachers for more information on specific, easy-to-use management plans.)

Among the topics usually found in the basic management plans of experienced teachers are tardies and attendance, late work, and expectations for appropriate behavior. Certain disciplines may require attention to other types of behavior; for example, a science teacher may wish to delineate specific rules for lab day, or the wood shop teacher for running certain types of equipment. Mentors should also remind beginning teachers that students' age level will also determine the rationale for a management plan. Rules appropriate to high school students may be unrealistic for younger children. Obviously, a "one size" plan does not fit all grades, disciplines, or teacher personalities.

Management plans should also specify what the consequences are when students do not adhere to the rules. Experienced teachers know that rules are pointless if they are not backed up by reasonable consequences. Has the new teacher planned what she will do if Sue leaves class to go to the bathroom without obtaining a hall pass from the teacher's desk? How will she handle Mark when he mysteriously appears at the class door thirty minutes after the bell has rung without a clear-cut explanation of where he has been? How will she respond when Betsy tries to turn in all her homework at the end of the grading quarter instead of when it was due? What will happen to Eugene's class standing if he misses four days this week and three days next week and the absences are not excused? Although we prefer not to detail specific consequences here, it is critical that you encourage new teachers to decide well in advance how they will respond to situations of this nature.

Although management systems should emphasize consistency, they should also allow for some flexibility. While some parts of the management plan require a common approach from situation to situation, some issues may have to be handled on a case-by-case basis. Even teachers who rigorously adhere to a policy of tardiness would not penalize two tardy students who brought a pass from their chemistry teacher explaining that they had been cleaning up after a lab. You might encourage your beginning teacher to be lenient with a student who was not able to finish a homework assignment because she was involved in a minor collision the night before or a student who ran to the bathroom without asking because she thought she was going to be sick. When working with less-experienced teachers, it is important to encourage them to be flexible. Without a plan, however, they will lack credibility and exceptions will become the norm.

A Teacher's Personality Will Influence His or Her Management Plan

We are all unique as people, so it is no surprise that we will also be unique as teachers. Some are extremely organized, while others thrive on piles of papers. Some feel that a fairly quiet classroom is necessary for student learning, while others positively enjoy an active, noisy environment. Some teachers prefer a highly structured classroom, while others may allow students to move from one activity to another without their intervention. Regardless of where you or your new colleague fall along this continuum, encourage new teachers to feel at ease with the plan they choose and let them know they have the right to structure the classroom in ways they feel appropriate to their needs and those of their students. Inexperienced teachers may find this difficult, especially if students complain, "Your class isn't as much fun as Mr. Villanueva's class because he lets us sit where we want and doesn't make us follow a seating chart" or "I can't even think in this class because it's too noisy." No one wants a situation that feels out of control, yet beginning teachers need to be reassured that pleasing all the students all the time is an impossible goal.

Classroom Management Involves Choosing One's Battles

An important instinct, but one that is difficult for new teachers, is knowing when to make an issue of student conduct. You notice that Barbie and Thad are having a conversation, but are they helping one another clarify the assignment or are they simply discussing their date for Friday night? The less-experienced teacher may jump on the situation immediately, discouraging productive student interaction, while the more experienced teacher recognizes that this conversation will be short-lived and can be safely ignored. If the students are chatting about after-school plans, the new teacher may inadvertently create a greater problem by making too big an issue of the conversation, forcing the students to stand up for themselves in front of their peers—a no-win situation. In the classrooms of experienced teachers, students will often sense when the teacher is moving forward with the lesson and self-correct.

Student behavior can be frustrating, but experienced teachers know that displays of teacher anger, sarcasm, or irritation with the class are almost always counterproductive. Humor is often a far more effective way to resolve management issues before they become significant problems. Unfortunately, new teachers find it difficult to relax enough in the classroom to take full advantage of this strategy. They fear that laughing with students will be seen as a sign of weakness or that the class will dissolve into chaos if they are not vigilant. However, you probably know from your own experience that humor, sometimes at your own expense, can create a pleasant, even affectionate atmosphere in the classroom. For example, a teacher can choose to be offended when a student walks in and says, "I was absent yesterday. Did we do anything?" or he may choose to respond with a little humor. "Nope, we held our breath waiting for you to return." New teachers need to learn that they don't need an elephant gun to swat every mosquito that buzzes!

Classroom Disruptions, the Bane of Management Plans

Unfortunately, schools are prime places for interruptions and distractions. Attendance collection, assemblies, intercom messages from the office, fire drills, a visit from the vice-principal to retrieve Billy for absences in the first semester—these are the annoyances all of us deal with when we work in a school setting. While experienced teachers learn to take these disruptions in stride, a newer teacher's tenuous control of the class may be jeopardized by everyday interruptions and distractions. There is no way to prevent these occurrences, but you can recommend a few helpful strategies. One teacher keeps a Do Not Disturb sign handy and hangs it on her door on those days when tests or student presentations make interruptions particularly inconvenient. Office staff may also be amenable to a teacher request to limit the number of messages delivered by intercom or student aide.

Nevertheless, some disruptions will occur. Encourage new teachers to stay focused on the business at hand so they can pick up exactly where they left off. If they can do this, students will not have time to go off-task and the lesson can proceed.

Special Students in Our Classrooms

Juan, a first-year third-grade teacher, really likes Matt, one of his students. Matt is creative, intelligent, and compassionate, and Juan knows that his high energy and inability to focus are because he has attention deficit hyperactive disorder (ADHD). Surprising noises erupt from Matt's side of the room, and he seems unable to sit in his seat for more than five minutes. When Juan can find time to give Matt individual attention, his student thrives academically. But when Matt works unaided, his progress is slow because he is so easily distracted. And when Matt loses focus, he sometimes disrupts the class. Juan's concern about the educational progress of Matt and his classmates puts him in a difficult position.

Managing this type of situation is very difficult for all teachers. Special needs students like Matt are not trying to be difficult, and teachers know they really should not be scolded for behavior they cannot always control. Furthermore, it is frustrating to realize that there is rarely enough time to give to either the special needs students or their classmates.

Obviously, encouraging the beginning teacher to ask the principal for help—in the form of an aide, a parent volunteer, or a reduction in class size—is a first step. Realistically, however, these solutions may be unavailable or impractical. When you are working with the beginning teacher, you might suggest these strategies:

1. Knowing as much as possible about students with special needs and their condition is essential. Counselors familiar with these students may be aware of strategies used successfully by previous teachers to encourage their educational progress. Parents can be invaluable resources because they have an in-depth knowledge of their own children. Students themselves often have some insight into their own needs, and bringing them into the conversation may help them take more responsibility for their actions. Finally, a teacher's observations should not be discounted; they often reveal specific areas of student strength and weakness.

2. The teacher should make students aware of the consistent daily routine or schedule in the classroom. Such routines provide an overall structure, and with this in place, students can anticipate daily procedures. Writing a daily agenda or schedule on the board, for example, assists students in maintaining their focus.

3. Beginning teachers should recognize that special needs students do better when the classroom routine includes a variety of activities. All students need some variety, but special needs students often have a short attention span. Alternating between quiet, desk-centered individual work and less-restrictive collaborative activities encourages student attention to the tasks at hand.

Working with the Hostile Student

Eva suspected that Cliff would be trouble from the first day of her student teaching. His cruel remarks, surly attitude, and teasing were clear indications that he had little regard for the feelings of his peers or his teachers. At first Eva couldn't pinpoint the reason for her uneasiness, because other students in the class often exhibited similar tendencies. But soon she noted that Cliff's remarks were more cutting than theirs, and that while other students laughed and apologized if peers called them on their remarks, Cliff glared at them until they dropped their eyes or turned away. Mac, Eva's cooperating teacher, was no more successful in deal-ing with Cliff's disdain for authority. The counselor described Cliff's family life as wildly dysfunctional and hinted that Cliff might also be abusing drugs. His behav-ior remained within the boundaries that allowed him to remain in school, but his grades were poor and his motivation worse.

Cliff is one of those students dreaded even by highly experienced and successful teachers, since his obvious hostility and misbehavior are rooted in situations beyond their control although they are the ones who must defuse the results. For inexperienced teachers, knowing when and how to defuse these situations can be extremely difficult. As the mentor, you might suggest some of the following strategies:

1. Encourage beginning teachers not to put themselves at risk. Though no one likes to think about the possibility of physical confrontation with students, it does occasion-ally happen. Hostile students, angry and upset about their life circumstances (often justifiably), can sometimes explode in aggressive and violent behavior; a teacher who gets in the way of such an eruption may be injured. Less-experienced teachers often hesitate to ask for assistance from the principal, counselor, or disciplinary officer because they feel it reflects poorly on their management skills. While understand-able, this attitude is unrealistic and has potentially dangerous consequences—some students have problems severe enough to challenge even a veteran teacher.

2. It is easy, but unwise, to react with hostility to students like Cliff. Confrontation simply provides an opportunity for more public manifestations of a hostile attitude. To put it bluntly, if a teacher backs a student like Cliff into a corner, Cliff will come out fighting, possibly literally, or at the very least, spouting a litany of verbal abuse. The secret to handling a student like Cliff is to correct him quietly and firmly but without anger or personal accusation. He needs to know that you will not tolerate disruptive behavior in the classroom, that he can decide how he will behave, and that you would prefer to keep him in the classroom if possible.

3. Bring Cliff's parents into the discussion. Although the counselor may be able to provide some insight into Cliff's behavior, his parents probably know him best and can give you additional information. They are also a source of support for your expectations about Cliff's behavior. Some parents may decline the invitation, but it is the teacher's obligation to at least extend it to them. Student teachers and less-experienced inservice teachers frequently dread parent contact because they feel they themselves may be blamed for students' misbehavior, but they need to understand that parental involvement is not an option but a necessary course when serious problems arise.

(For additional information on how to work with at-risk students, see Chapter 7 in *Mentoring Across Boundaries: Helping Beginning Teachers Succeed in Challenging Situations* [Stenhouse]).

✎ · Summary · ✎

"Ms. Dryden, I'm just letting you know that Marty will be out of your class for the next three days; he'll have in-school suspension with me in the office," announced Principal Hendricks.

Sarah felt a pang of guilty relief at the news. Marty had caused endless problems throughout the semester in her third-period history class, and yesterday he had crossed all the lines when he threw a weighted ballpoint pen across the room at another student. Fortunately, he had missed the student but hit the blackboard, shattering a large section of it. She was pleased not to have to deal with him for a few days but worried about his eventual return.

Like Sarah, most teachers quickly realize that, although they value the temporary intervention of an administrator, their management problems will not disappear permanently as a result. Mentors can remind beginning teachers that they can expect students like Marty to continue to challenge them. It is essential that teachers learn the management strategies that work best for them.

Management problems will always require attention, but mentors can reassure new colleagues that these problems are not a reason for teacher embarrassment. Given the wrong combination of students or circumstances, any teacher may experience management problems. In mentoring a beginning teacher, remind her that investing the time to sort out management procedures is worth it. When teachers don't have to worry about student behavior, they can concentrate on those aspects of learning that are more enjoyable to everyone.

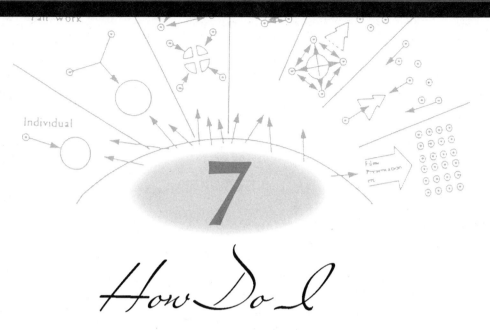

7

How Do I

ENCOURAGE TEACHERS WHO WORK WITH ENGLISH LANGUAGE LEARNERS?

Mentoring new teachers is a privilege and an obligation for experienced teachers, the currency in which we pay our dues to the profession we love. It offers an opportunity to multiply our hard-won knowledge about education by sharing what we have learned with newcomers to the field. Most of us recognize the importance of informing, supporting, and encouraging new colleagues, whether they are student teachers or simply new to our districts. Generally speaking, the more challenging the teaching task for the newcomer, the more essential the role of the mentor. This brings us to the topic of the present chapter, for few content areas can rival the teaching of English language learners for challenge, complexity, and uncertainty. Consequently, few content areas have a more critical need for mentors.

If ours were a perfect world, all teachers who mentor new professionals who work with English language learners would have ELL teaching experience themselves. However, in the world of real districts, real schools, and real schedules, mentors assigned to work with these new professionals may teach in different content areas or at different age levels. This does not automatically mean that the partnership between mentor and mentee cannot be productive, for many of the issues the ELL teacher faces are common to any teaching situation and are not related to language acquisition. The goal of this chapter is to provide basic language teaching information that will stimulate the thinking and inform the practice of mentors who may or may not teach English language learners themselves. We begin with accounts of three situations in which mentoring or its absence was influential in the professional development of the new teachers involved.

✎ · Teacher Stories · ✎

Student Teacher Shelby Dunstan

Ever since Shelby Dunstan decided on education as a career, she knew the population with whom she hoped to work: English language learners. As a child, she had been touched by the language-related struggles of her own mother, an immigrant from China. After her college training in English Education and TESL, Shelby began her student teaching at Wilderness Middle School in a southwestern state.

Wilderness had begun developing its program for ELLs eighteen years before Shelby's arrival and had earned state and national recognition for excellence. The well-organized TESL curriculum was written specifically for the district by a team of teachers experienced with students who are learning English, and a responsive, helpful, easy-to-administer battery of precourse and postcourse assessment tools was also in place to document student progress in a clear, logical manner. Local district policy mandated no more than fifteen students in ELL courses, giving Shelby and her mentor, Marisol Torres, a total student load of just seventy-four individuals. Marisol made the state standards available to Shelby early in the semester.

Over the course of the semester, the two teachers became close personal friends and supportive professional allies. The school encouraged both teachers to attend district and statewide TESL conferences together during the student teaching semester to meet other professionals and discuss their experiences and techniques. Though Shelby faced all the typical new-teacher challenges during her student teaching, and a few unique challenges specifically related to her ELLs, the support of both Marisol and Wilderness's excellent program helped her end the semester successfully. She felt proud to be beginning the life she'd envisioned as a TESL professional, and she looked forward to her permanent placement in a nearby district.

New Teacher Brett Allen

When Brett Allen began teaching a high school class for English language learners at City Center High School in an urban Arizona district, it was due to administrative circumstances rather than choice. The tenth-grade honors class he had been prepared and excited to teach had an enrollment of just nine students, and the school administration could not justify such a small student-teacher ratio in a mainstream classroom. The course was cancelled, students were rescheduled, and second-year teacher Brett was tapped to take over a class of ELLs.

Because he taught at a school in which nearly half the students were Native American or Hispanic, Brett had previously considered becoming TESL certified, but as he investigated the requirements and the district's TESL program itself, he decided that the program and its target population were not for him. Although still theoretically willing to "teach anyone, anywhere, anytime," Brett had decided that his true interests and aptitudes were at odds with his idealism and best intentions. Personally and professionally, he was more interested in other pursuits.

When his principal approached him about the assignment change, however, he felt he had no choice but to agree. Normally a confident and highly motivated young professional, Brett was intimidated by the prospect of jumping into the ELL arena. Several other teachers in the English department had also been recruited to teach ELLs, and Brett had heard few good things about his colleagues' experiences. The curriculum had been adopted from another district and seemed to be a poor fit; attempts to refine it had led to confusion rather than improvement. No systematic student assessment had been done, and none was planned. Resources—even basic textbooks—were virtually nonexistent, leaving teachers of ELLs with the time-draining responsibility of writing their own materials daily. Brett had been told that the students, especially the boys, lacked intellectual curiosity and motivation. Parental involvement was reputed to be negligible, and school administrators adopted a laissez-faire attitude while still expecting documented results.

As a relatively new teacher eager to prove himself at City Center, Brett also felt uncertain about asking for help or advice from other teachers for fear of looking as if he didn't know what he was doing. Collaboration with other teachers was very rare at City Center, and conversations about ELL classes consisted of complaining or guardedness. Significantly, the school did not assign a mentor to Brett because he was no longer a first-year teacher, and this omission left Brett without adequate support.

The first weeks of Brett's English 2 class, designed to transition students rapidly into mainstream English courses, did little to alleviate his fears. English 2 was the smallest class in his schedule with fifteen students, but it was by far the most complex. After the first day, he realized that the Native American students had radically different needs and concerns from their Hispanic classmates. Some students were highly intelligent and struggling only with language acquisition, while others appeared to have low ability or even, perhaps, undiagnosed learning disabilities or behavior problems in addition to their limited English. It was immediately obvious to Brett that individualized, differentiated instruction would be essential, but because resources were largely unavailable, Brett could see that lesson planning for such instruction would be inordinately time consuming in his busy teacher's life.

It is a tribute to Brett's own motivation, professionalism, and concern that his students still made good progress during that year, and a respectable percentage of them transitioned successfully into the mainstream classroom following his instruction. However, unlike Shelby, Brett concluded his school year with diminished enthusiasm for teaching overall and a definitely reduced willingness to work with ELLs in the future.

Experienced Teacher Melinda Montgomery

Melinda Montgomery, an experienced fourth-grade teacher who specialized in math and science content in college, had been working happily at Maplevale Elementary School in her suburban Wisconsin school district for fourteen years. As is true in many districts across the United States, the composition of her classes was gradually changing year by year with the steady influx of Hmong, Hispanic, Asian, and East Indian students. They came to the district for one of several reasons. Some families owned or worked on nearby farms. Others arrived because of their parents' employment at a large nearby medical clinic. Still others were the children of business owners. Most were not recent immigrants; in fact, many of the students from these groups had been born in the United States. In social interactions in the classroom, the children responded well to Melinda. They seemed cooperative and sometimes shared information about their own cultural backgrounds, which Melinda encouraged and the other students enjoyed greatly.

When it came to written work and reading comprehension, however, Melinda noticed an achievement gap. These children of immigrant families were simply not reading or writing as well as their oral language suggested they should be, even though some had been in American schools all their academic lives. Melinda tried hard to help them with extra attention and special assistance, but she became increasingly frustrated by their negligible progress. Finally, a fellow teacher suggested that she discuss the situation with a district ELL resource teacher.

Melinda did not consider herself an ELL teacher, since all the children in her classroom spoke English fluently, nor did she think of mentoring as an option at first, since she was a veteran teacher herself. However, she was puzzled enough to seek the support she needed. Later, she told her principal how grateful she was for the referral. "The ELL resource teacher mentored me for the rest of the school year, and she made an incredible difference. I understand the basic information about these students and the pace of their acquisition of English so much better. We even discussed my frequent feelings of inadequacy when working with them," Melinda told the principal. "I feel as if I know what to do now."

· ✄ · ✄ · ✄ ·

Mentoring assistance can be a critical factor in professional success for a student teacher like Shelby, a newer teacher like Brett, or an experienced teacher like Melinda. For example, Shelby's natural abilities and college training were similar to Brett's, yet Shelby spent an enriching and largely happy semester under Marisol's mentorship while Brett struggled alone with overwork, exhaustion, and self-doubt to teach a class for which he was poorly prepared. If there had been a mentor to listen, encourage, and advise, Brett's commitment to teaching and his strong natural abilities might have led to a much more successful outcome. Brett's story, unfortunately, is an unhappily common one among teachers of English language learners.

Every content area, including ELL teaching, has unique concerns. A mentor who comes from another content area will find background information helpful in assisting mentees working with second language learners. The following background information is obviously limited, but it may provide a starting point for further investigation of the field.

What Mentors Should Know About English Language Teaching

Mentors should know that extra mentoring time may be needed for new teachers of ELLs who lack sufficient training in the field. Shelby's success at Wilderness resulted from a combination of factors—good academic preparation, a stable program within the district, and excellent mentoring. Many new teachers of ELLs do not have her advantages and must begin teaching English language learners without adequate training or support. Brett found himself teaching ELLs with little prior preparation and relatively meager interest in the field, simply because circumstances in his school dictated that he do so. Sadly, his experience is not unique.

Many positive changes have taken place in the field over the past two decades, sometimes including mandated training for teachers in all content areas who work in districts with high numbers of English language learners. University programs in English Education now routinely offer courses leading to state TESL certification. Some districts have responded to the negative experiences of previous teachers by ensuring that classes with high percentages of ELLs are taught by the best-trained teachers available. All of these changes are very positive. However, the assumption that anyone who speaks English can easily move to teaching it also remains widely held by school administrators. An experienced teacher of English language learners recently quipped, "We don't think anyone who has a brain is qualified to do brain surgery, but people will tell you seriously that anyone who speaks English can teach it."

One of the most significant roles of mentors in any content area is to keep beginning teachers growing in both their professional skills and their enthusiasm for teaching. Teachers with inadequate preparation can easily come to feel inept and discouraged when working with English language learners. Early in the partnership, a mentor should determine whether the new teacher has had relevant training or experience in the field. If not, extra mentoring time may be needed.

Mentors should be aware that teachers of English language learners often fill the additional role of advocates for their students. Although all teachers should be advocates for their students, ELLs may have special needs in this area. Whether in a separate class, a pullout program, or a mainstream course offering, the language teacher is frequently the first person at school whom ELLs come to trust deeply. Consequently, the language teacher often becomes the resource to whom students bring their specific questions and concerns. Students ask how their family's electric bills are to be paid, how their mothers can get driver's licenses, what their math teacher means by "percentage," and numerous other puzzling matters. This type of interaction is usually very rewarding, but it also translates into an additional commitment of time and care for the teacher. Mentors for these teachers should be aware of the dual role their mentees often play and should encourage them to care for themselves as well as their students.

Mentors should know that ELLs are sometimes inadvertently misevaluated for placement by teachers and school officials. As Brett discovered at City Center, administrators or teachers who must make placement decisions for new ELLs sometimes fail to suspect that a particular student has learning disabilities or serious emotional problems along with underdeveloped language skills. Atypical behavior in these cases is often assumed to relate exclusively to language issues, which may not be correct, for ELLs have the same range of learning strengths and complexities as their mainstream contemporaries.

In addition, students who have lived in the United States for several years may speak English so fluently that they are also frequently misplaced because of their own verbal ability. Despite inadequate reading comprehension and writing ability, their fluency in spoken English may cause them to be placed in mainstream classes with no support, where they puzzle teachers like Melinda. Later, these students are sometimes mistakenly diagnosed as being learning disabled due to the gap between their social and academic language, when in fact they are simply developing their academic skills more slowly than their interpersonal ones, as is quite normal for English language learners.

Placement of students in ELL classes is an inexact undertaking. If mentees express concerns that some of their students seem to be incorrectly placed, mentors are wise to take those concerns seriously, because misplacement often does happen in this field, despite the best efforts of those who assess the students initially.

Mentors should know that developmental timetables for social language and academic language differ significantly. Elementary teacher Melinda Montgomery first met with her district ELL specialist, Susan Diaz, because she noticed a striking gap between her students' relatively good use of conversational English and their lesser mastery of reading and writing.

"When I work with these kids, I realize how much I personally thrive on the steady progress of my students," Melinda told Susan. "I don't seem to get anywhere with these particular children, though. We get along well; I love them just like I love all the students in my class. That's not the problem. But they seem impervious to improvement. The other students fly, while these students creep along. What am I doing wrong here?"

First described by University of Toronto teacher and researcher Jim Cummins, the distinction between Basic Interpersonal Communication Skills (BICS) and Cognitive Academic Language Proficiency (CALP) has helped teachers understand student performance of the type Melinda saw in her class. "Despite teacher observation that peer-appropriate conversational fluency in English developed rapidly, a period of 5–7 years was required, on average, for immigrant students to approach grade norms in academic aspects of English" (Cummins 2003). In short, students learn to converse in English quickly, but academic language proficiency takes much longer to develop.

Mentors should recognize that student levels in ELL classes are likely to be even more diverse than in the mainstream classroom and that accommodating that diversity will increase the time demands for their mentees. Differing student ability levels are typical in any classroom, of course, regardless of age or subject matter. By nature, students are unique human beings, and their abilities vary. However, ELLs struggle with differences on two levels: the differences in ability that are unique to the students themselves and the differences in students' prior exposure to English.

ELLs language acquisition in their lives beyond the classroom is often uneven and may differ dramatically from student to student. For example, one high school student, who works in the kitchen at a large hotel part time, can amaze her teacher and dazzle her classmates with her sophisticated vocabulary whenever the subject involves food or cooking. The same student may be completely unfamiliar with the vocabulary used in a medical office. Her classmate, whose mother is a physician, can discuss medical issues with ease but knows nothing at all about food. A third rebuilds cars as a hobby and is widely familiar with the vocabulary of that field but few others. Diagnosing student knowledge and planning lessons for a class with such varying needs is part of the special challenge of teaching English language learners.

Mentors should know that teaching ELLs and grading their work rank among the most time-consuming and energy-draining teaching assignments in any district. Even at well-organized Wilderness, Shelby spent unexpectedly long hours rewriting course materials to address her students' needs specifically. Because Brett's school had far fewer resources than Shelby's, Brett's job was even more difficult. He found himself writing entirely new materials for his ELL class day after day—for several ability levels. Though all teaching takes time to prepare adequately, the number of preparation hours worked by new ELL teachers like Brett might astonish teachers in other content areas. Grading, with its need for complex error analysis in student work, can also take lots of time.

Although Melinda's students comprehended spoken English nearly as well as native speakers, she found that she needed to break longer written assignments into smaller, highly focused segments for them. Fortunately, Melinda had years of teaching experience and a well-stocked filing cabinet to aid this process, but new teachers may be inexperienced at writing curriculum and have few resources beyond what is available in their buildings. Mentors should not assume that the number of hours their mentees report spending on class preparation is exaggerated; adequate preparation for their classes can be discouragingly time consuming.

Mentors should know that ELLs will usually maintain powerful ties to other cultures. Teachers must learn to understand these cultures, exhibit respect for them, and value the languages associated with them if students are to feel at home in the classroom. Students who sense that their teachers value their prior knowledge and experiences tend to be more willing to cooperate with classroom plans. However, when language is a barrier, teachers may need to go outside the classroom and the students themselves to learn about these cultures. In a school term laden with multiple demands, new teachers may decide that this is a step that can be omitted.

Professional experience suggests otherwise. Especially in the upper grades, students who feel marginalized by a lack of interest or a devaluation of their heritage cultures, prior knowledge, and potential contributions are far more likely to oppose the classroom program and become behavior problems. When students feel accepted and respected in their school, they identify with its goals and engage in the process of learning. Conversely, oppositional behavior is likely when students feel that they are not understood and valued by their teachers. Mentors can join their mentees in learning about students' cultural backgrounds and encourage mentees to take the needed time for this project.

Mentors should investigate state and national standards for ELLs with their mentees. Obviously, the mentor and the mentee must work within existing state and national standards and assessment schemes. In some cases, standards are realistic and very helpful to teachers. In other districts, instructional life is complicated by unrealistic or even punitive standards for English language learners. For example, no special accommodations are made for ELLs in standards testing in some regions, regardless of their language abilities, and the scores of these students may not be separated from those of native speakers for analysis. Whatever the case in a particular locale, it is crucial that both mentoring partners understand district ELL goals and how they will be assessed. Mentors should assist their new colleagues in determining the impact of state and national assessments upon instructional decisions.

Mentors should remember that both new and experienced teachers who feel inadequate in their work may hesitate to ask for help. While by no means limited to English language teaching, this factor certainly applies to teachers of ELLs. Many teachers, including new professionals, may feel that they are grappling in a fog of inexperience, limited resources, and perplexing student challenges. Yet, like Brett, they worry about their professional reputations if they appear to need help. The mentor here must be tactfully proactive to become a safe confidant and advisor, the initiator of discussion, the raiser of issues. A good mentor allows the new teacher the freedom to risk telling the truth, asking questions, and receiving vital encouragement.

✄ · Questions Encountered by ELL Mentors · ✄

Question: *I'm teaching a mostly ELL fourth-grade class. It's nearly Christmas, and I really don't see much progress. Is that typical?*

Sometimes, the soldiers in the trenches cannot see the overall progress of the war. Your immediate battle may be with discouragement. Most teachers who work with English language learners, like most teachers in other content areas, are doing an excellent, though not perfect, job for their students. Undoubtedly, progress is being made.

Question: *I hope you're right—but I'd like to know for sure. How can I tell if students really are progressing?*

When student progress is slow, it may be invisible to either the teacher or the students themselves from one assignment to the next. Keeping thorough files of student work and observing and tracking classroom contributions are not only important ingredients for grading and placement decisions, but they also allow both students and teachers to see positive changes taking place over time.

Question: *Am I making my classes too easy or even too hard for my ELLs? How can I tell?*

Although ELLs have limited language skills, which may impact either their comprehension or productive activities, it's important to recognize that they have the same intellectual abilities as their mainstream classmates. Teachers need to keep student expectations high enough to challenge and interest the students. Sympathy for the plight of language learners is appropriate, but schoolwork must also push students slightly. Teachers who expect their students to do poorly are seldom disappointed, but fortunately, the reverse is also true.

Question: *I'm the only teacher in my building working with ELLs, and I feel pretty isolated. How can I find others with whom I can share information?*

Start by contacting other public or private schools in your district with programs for ELLs. Your district office can put you in touch with them, or you can go directly to the schools and inquire at their offices. Teachers need each other for the exchange of ideas, materials, problem solving, and emotional support.

Question: *Are there good professional organizations with which I could affiliate?*

Several, actually! Probably the best known of these is TESOL (Teachers of English to Speakers of Other Languages). TESOL has reasonable membership rates for teachers and offers an enormous amount of material through both their electronic and print resources. State and regional meetings and conferences are well publicized and frequent. Larger cities may have citywide groups as well.

Question: *I teach in a small town that does not have a professional library. How can I find resources to help me?*

Whether or not your district maintains a good library of resources for English language teaching, an unprecedented quantity of material is now available to teachers. By all means, seek out the many resources available online. Immediately useful age- and ability-graded activities for the classroom are plentiful if you find and bookmark suitable sites. It is not necessary in every case to reinvent the curriculum day by day. There are numerous sites for student practice online, too.

Question: *I would like to learn more about the cultures of my ELL students. What's the best way to do this?*

Print and online resources will provide much helpful information about your students' cultures, but contact with parents, grandparents, and other representatives of those cultures may open the doors of knowledge even further. Linguistic and cultural groups in almost all districts have individuals who can speak and comprehend English well enough to be good informants; seek them out in your area. They are usually willing to help an interested teacher to better serve the needs of their culture's children in the classroom.

Question: *Help! I have just learned that I'll be teaching a high school reading and writing class for English language learners. I've never done this before— what's first?*

As a general rule, begin with students, not curriculum. If good assessment practices are in place for ELLs in your district, you can go to the school files to uncover information about your students' strengths and needs; that is, of course, the most precise way to determine student ability levels. However, if the district or building offers no assessment or inadequate assessment, conduct informal evaluations of your students early in the school year. For an elementary teacher, basic one-on-one conversational interactions, plus asking the student to read aloud and respond to simple questions about the reading in a nonthreatening setting, can reveal enough about the student's current English skills to permit better planning on the teacher's part. Asking students to narrate a wordless picture book can also be appropriate for elementary or middle school students. Older students can be given a simple writing task on an age-appropriate topic along with some brief oral interview questions. Try to keep the questions reading-related, not personal, since students may have already learned how to respond to personal questions in English with deceptive ease. While not thoroughly scientific, even this basic type of classroom research can give you a clear beginning place as you plan lessons. The vital point is that teachers must know their students' needs at least approximately before they can prepare appropriate instruction. Too many new teachers simply take whatever books are on hand and begin with Chapter 1, regardless of student needs; this is particularly unfortunate for ELLs.

Question: *What kinds of classroom practices will help my ELL third graders feel part of my mixed-ability class?*

ELLs may fail to comprehend what is said in their classrooms at first, but they are reassured and encouraged when they can participate in repeated classroom routines. If you consistently collect and distribute papers in the same manner, use the same classroom phrases regularly, illustrate the procedures for turning in make-up work, and generally give clear instructions as to classroom behavior, ELLs quickly come to succeed in these tasks as well as their mainstream classmates do. Procedures matter greatly in a classroom with nonnative speakers, even if the students are in the upper grades. An added benefit of predictable classroom practices is the accompanying reduction in student misbehavior. ELLs students like to know what to expect and feel most secure in predictable settings. Furthermore, predictable routines appeal to native speakers as well.

Question: *I teach high school ELLs, and I noticed that they sometimes get lost partway through the class. What can I do to prevent this problem?*

Good practice for language learners in many cases is simply good classroom practice taken to a slightly higher level and used more consistently. Several techniques that help ELL students comprehend the lesson content and lesson progress are discussed below, but they are by no means the only ones.

The first helpful technique for English language teachers is to form the habit of clearly marking the transition from one part of each lesson to another. Experienced teachers know that when they conclude one activity or portion of a class and begin another, they should make an explicit transition so the class understands what is happening. This practice is especially vital to students who are nonnative speakers of English.

Second, students often lose the flow of a lesson when they encounter unfamiliar vocabulary. Noting and preteaching vocabulary that will be encountered in any new lesson, reading, or activity will often pay large dividends of student interest, comprehension, and ability to complete assignments.

One of the helpful roles that a mentor can play in assisting mentees who work with language learners is to observe their classes to offer feedback regarding teacher practices that may be confusing or frustrating to ELLs. One area of possible confusion is rate of speech. Some English speakers speak more quickly than others by nature and habit; this obviously has the potential to cause difficulty for students. However, an English language learner must learn to adapt to a range of normal rates of speech—even rapid speech. One practical technique teachers can employ instead of unduly slowing their speech is to continue to speak at the rate that is normal for them, but pause longer between sentences to give students a chance to catch up with the message. Reiterating an idea a second or even third time in a slightly different form is also helpful; a student may be confused by one way of expressing an idea but may understand the concept clearly when it is re-phrased. Conveniently, these techniques help native speakers of English, too; they are good educational practice in any classroom but are more essential in classes with nonnative speakers.

Finally, English language learners are often thrown off course by teachers who interrupt their own speech with side comments and sentence restarts. During Shelby's student teaching at Wilderness, Marisol noticed her habit of commenting on her own statements and then restarting or restructuring sentences. With Shelby's permission, Marisol videotaped one of Shelby's middle school ELL classes. Shelby was surprised to watch the tape and hear her own stream of speech. One portion went as follows:

> Okay, group, on Thursday, at least if everything goes as it should, we will be finish-ing our unit on… no, not Thursday, I mean Tuesday. I don't know why I always say Thursday when I mean Tuesday, sorry. Anyway, on Tuesday, we'll be finishing our grammar unit, and then we're going to do something you'll really enjoy. Well, I hope you enjoyed the grammar unit, too, but…

Shelby shook her head as she watched the videotape. "Oh, no! I'm all over the place; I don't even finish one thought before I'm off on another one. No wonder the students get confused sometimes." Marisol assured her that most speakers do the same thing in normal conversation but that it might be a good habit to break for her ELL classes.

✂ · Summary · ✂

The background and suggestions provided in this chapter provide only a small glimpse of the concerns and issues that impact this complex field for ELL teachers, their mentors, and their students. Mentors need to realize that extra mentoring time is required to help beginning teachers become advocates for their English language learners, recognize appropriate evaluation tools, and acknowledge the differences in students' developmental timetables and levels. Mentors can encourage new teachers to help students maintain their cultural ties, to keep abreast of state and national standards, and to feel free to request help.

Fortunately, the teaching of English language learners has received so much attention in recent years that it is not difficult to find further information on specific topics of interest. Though few areas of teaching are more complex, those teachers who have consistently worked with nonnative speakers can affirm that few areas offer more rewards in cross-cultural awareness, professional challenge, and deep interpersonal relationships with students and their families. Being mentored by a caring and helpful colleague may be the most significant factor allowing the new teacher of ELLs to move from uncertainty, difficulty, and tentative instruction to assurance, confidence, and high-quality work. It's a job worth doing.

The authors gratefully acknowledge Brad Kamradt for his contributions to this chapter.

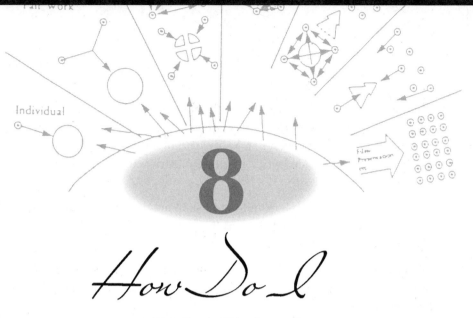

8

How Do I

HELP INTEGRATE BEGINNING TEACHERS INTO THE SCHOOL CULTURE?

Teachers new to a school building must quickly learn the culture and the related nuances that go along with the singular and collective personalities of the staff. A school's culture can have a direct effect on a first-year teacher's experience.

— **Rob Danin and Margaret A. Bacon,** *A Better Beginning*

"Who am I? How do I fit in?" Just as many students ask these questions during their adolescent maturation, so, too, beginning teachers often wonder, "Am I really a teacher? Is teaching a good career fit for me? How do I fit into this school system?" Each teacher possesses an individual personality, and each school district—and even each school building, grade level, interdisciplinary team, or academic department—displays individual strengths, moods, biases, and perhaps even quirks! Mentors can help beginning teachers navigate this new terrain by self-assessing the school environment or school culture and providing a picture of it to their mentees, introducing them to faculty and staff members, modeling respect for administrators, and following school procedures.

✎ · Self-Assessing the School Culture · ✎

Prior to thinking about how to discuss the school culture with the beginning teacher, the mentor may wish to make a school self-assessment using the following questions. The questions refer to "school," but depending on the size or emphasis in your specific situation, you may wish to substitute "grade level," "interdisciplinary team," "academic department," or "school district."

1. Examine your school mission and vision statements. What are the central beliefs of these statements? Are these beliefs truly a part of your school? How do you see these beliefs enacted in daily life?

2. What other beliefs do faculty in your school building display toward students? Toward student learning? Toward colleagues? What is your major emphasis in student learning?

3. What are typical instructional strategies used in your school? Do faculty prefer to use individual work, small-group work, large-group discussions, multimedia, lecture, or a variety of these methods?

4. What are typical assessments used in your school? Do faculty prefer quizzes and tests, projects and presentations, essays and rubrics, portfolios and reflections, or other assessments? What does this say about the beliefs of the faculty?

5. What is the school philosophy toward working with parents? Are parents viewed as an integral part of the school or as an important but outside influence?

6. How are professional development and school change viewed by the faculty? As a whole, would the faculty be characterized as early adopters, change agents, critical questioners, or late adopters? Does the faculty give greater value to innovation or tradition?

7. What is the leadership style of the administration? Do most changes occur in a top-down (administration-initiated), bottom-up (faculty-initiated), or collaborative (administration-faculty cooperation) mode?

8. How do faculty respond to each other? Do instructors tend to close their classroom doors and work individually, or are successes celebrated and problems solved as a group?

9. What is the general mood within the school: positive? enthusiastic? happy? neutral? pessimistic?

10. How would you characterize a typical hour within the teachers' lounge? Do teachers tend to be social on a polite or close-knit level? Do teachers tend to discuss students/

      parents/administrators positively or negatively? How often is laughter an integral part of a teacher's gathering?

11. How often do the personal and the professional merge? Do faculty members attend school events regularly? Do faculty intentionally see each other outside of school hours?

12. What is a continual problem that surfaces in the school? How does this problem help characterize the school?

13. What are the expectations for classroom management? How does the school system handle extreme classroom management situations?

After you, as the mentor, have assessed your school system, you will be more prepared to discuss the school environment with the beginning teacher. Be positive, poised, and professional by explaining the expectations, describing the hopes, and being frank but tactful when questioned.

✎ · Respecting the Beginning Teacher's Perspective · ✎

Some educators believe that school climate is evident within the first three to eight minutes of stepping into a school building. The welcome signs, signage for main office and restrooms, staff demeanor, students' passage in hallways, and hallway and restroom appearance all present a quick first impression of the school. As the mentor, you may wish to ask the beginning teacher for his or her first impressions prior to initiating a discussion about the school environment.

In the following scene, Rhonna explains her impression of the teacher's lounge and of a particularly irate teacher:

Rhonna: *I just came from the teacher's lounge, and I couldn't believe what was happening.*

Elyse: *Tell me about it.*

Rhonna: *Well, usually people are talking about the weather or a sports event in quiet conversations. But today Mr. Blarsby came in, threw his books on the table, and started yelling profanities about a student in his class.*

Elyse: *What had happened?*

Rhonna: *I guess the student didn't have his work done, Mr. Blarsby yelled at him, the student yelled back, and he told the student to go to the principal's office. The student refused to go, so Mr. Blarsby called the main office and asked Mrs. Miller to come to his room to get the student. After Mr. Blarsby made the phone call, the student yelled more profanities and then walked out of the classroom and out of the school.*

Elyse: *What happened next?*

Rhonna: *Mr. Blarsby said Mrs. Miller told him she would contact the parents and would talk to the student after he returned and had calmed down. Mr. Blarsby was so angry he was calling the student names, throwing his books, and stomping around the teachers' lounge. Even his hands were shaking.*

Elyse: *It sounds like he was pretty upset.*

Rhonna: *Yeah, but I didn't like how he was handling it. He seemed to be just as immature as the students.*

Elyse: *Sometimes teachers view the teachers' lounge as a safety zone where they can release their feelings and frustrations so they can return to the classroom in a calmer mood.*

Rhonna: *Well, I didn't return in a calmer mood! I was having a good day until I heard him ranting and raving.*

Elyse: *The mood of the teachers' lounge varies from school to school. In my last school, the teachers always brought treats to share, they asked about each other's families, and there was constant laughter.*

Rhonna: *I don't think that describes this teachers' lounge.*

Elyse: *[laughs] No, sometimes it doesn't. When I first came here, I was shocked—like you—at how negative some teachers were. I decided to avoid the teachers' lounge completely. Then I decided that that was just avoiding the problem and that I wasn't part of the solution.*

Rhonna: *So what did you do?*

Elyse: *I now do a "walk-through" every day. I walk into the lounge, speak to people using their first names, find something positive to say, get a cup of coffee, and walk out.*

Rhonna: *Is it hard to always be positive?*

Elyse: *Oh, not really. If Sid, the basketball coach, is reading the sports section, I find something good to say about the last game, the next game, the new uniforms, or a specific player. If Marilou is there, I ask about her garden or how her son is doing at college. Maya and Stuart are both film buffs, so I often ask about a specific film or for a video recommendation.*

Rhonna: *I get it. You try to make the lounge a more positive place.*

Elyse: *Yes, I try to control it instead of letting it control me. [Laughs] Sometimes it's hard. One of the teachers who is now retired used to be very grumpy. If I said, "It's going to be a sunny day," she would reply, "Yes, but it probably won't last long." That used to really upset me until I decided to make it into a game. I tried to see if I could coax her into saying something positive! If not, I'd just walk out and laugh internally. I decided I couldn't let one person ruin my day.*

Rhonna: *So what would you have done if you had heard Mr. Blarsby explode?*

Elyse: *I might stay long enough to say, "I'm sorry that you had a bad day. I hope the rest of your day goes better." Then I'd walk out. It depends, though. Sometimes people just need someone to listen to them and empathize with the situation.*

Rhonna: *Thanks. I might try some of those things. While I'm driving home today, I'll try to think of something positive that I could say to some of the teachers.*

Elyse: *That's a great plan!*

✇ · Introducing the Faculty and Staff · ✇

As a mentor, you can help acquaint the beginning teacher with the school culture by introducing your colleague to faculty and staff. Be sure to start with your team or department, the colleagues with whom the beginning teacher will have the most interaction. Then progress to other important personnel, such as guidance counselors, librarians, special education faculty and aides, ELL teachers, and other faculty. The secretaries and custodians also deserve immediate introductions since all teachers know that they often prove to be the best allies in providing assistance. As you are talking, try using the first names of both individuals multiple times to aid each person in remembering the other's name in the next encounter. To help the new teacher remember all of these individuals, mentors might create pages of photos and names, possibly from a yearbook or website.

After getting to know the teachers by name, the next step is to help the beginning teacher locate people who may be informal mentors: those of similar age and experience, teaching styles, or philosophies. Experienced teachers realize that knowing students on an individual basis often promotes more student motivation; similarly, becoming better acquainted with faculty can aid our own interactions, as shown by the following scene that Adela relates to Ricardo:

One year I hated taking my fifth graders to the computer lab because Margie, the computer lab instructor, showed little patience and often yelled at my students. I didn't know how to handle this, so I asked Mrs. Williams, our principal, for advice. She listened and then said, "I think you need to get to know Margie better." I couldn't believe it! I expected Mrs. Williams to tell me how to approach Margie about her teaching, or I thought Mrs. Williams would volunteer to talk to Margie herself. I was completely floored. I thanked her and walked out of the office, thinking that had been a waste of my time.

But since I didn't want to talk to Margie about her poor teaching, I decided to try Mrs. Williams's advice. Each day I found a few moments before school, during lunch, or after school to talk briefly with Margie. Once after I asked if Margie had seen a certain TV program, she told me that she couldn't watch TV because her husband badly needed a kidney transplant and she spent her evenings and weekends taking care of him. When I learned this, my attitude changed. I realized that I had judged too quickly. I now understood that Margie's lack of patience with the students was simply a release of her own pent-up emotions.

When Margie's husband died a few weeks later, the other teachers and I provided support for Margie. We took food to her house, attended the funeral, and did other things for her, but I think what she appreciated the most was that when she returned to school, one of us would stop by her room and just listen to her as we grieved together. And an amazing thing happened. Because she no longer had this tense life of worrying about her husband, she became a calmer, more patient teacher. I realized that Mrs. Williams was right. I did need to get to know Margie better. And that's probably true of many situations. I learned that we can't make assumptions and that we should tread lightly and get to know others.

Mentors can show beginning teachers that many conflicts of interest can be resolved by simply getting to know others. Mentors can be role models of good listening, as shown by the following scenario:

"Wow, that was one long meeting!" Nancy declared to her mentor, as they exited a committee meeting in which teachers debated whether grade-level teams or "techie" teachers should be the first ones to receive Smart Boards in their classrooms.

Steve smiled. "Well, I'd rather have one long meeting that is calm than have one with people yelling. Sometimes people only keep repeating the same arguments, so I tried to get them to listen to each other."

"Uh, huh," Nancy said. "I noticed that you asked a lot of questions."

"Yes, I wanted everyone to have an opportunity to express their views and for us to see the pros and cons to each method."

Mentors can role model being a questioner and listener during staff or committee meetings, and they can encourage the beginning teacher to speak during these meetings:

"But, I noticed that you didn't join the discussion, Nancy. Were you unsure about your own opinions or were you unwilling to talk in front of such a large group?"

"Oh, I thought the teams should receive the Smart Boards. That's what happened during my practicum, and the ones who were knowledgeable about technology taught the others on the team."

"That's an important point. You had an experience that you could have shared with the group. I hope you share your experiences next time."

Sometimes staff meetings or committee meetings can be overwhelming for the "new kid on the block." Mentors can encourage beginning teachers to feel comfortable in these situations by getting to know the other faculty, listening to others, and not feeling afraid to speak. Often beginning teachers have had practicum experiences in multiple school districts, possess more technological background, and have seen experimental programs in practice. Once the new teacher speaks at a faculty gathering, perhaps with the mentor's encouragement, she will be more likely to share her opinions and receive the respect of other faculty members.

✑ · Modeling Respect for Administrators · ✑

Often beginning teachers will share administrative gripes or concerns with a mentor or team mentors. While it's easy to blame others, mentors often need to show that teachers should respect the position the administrator holds. When Carlotta, a new fourth-grade teacher, complained that the principal had criticized her for not being in the hallway between classes, Francie told her the following story:

I realize that you were probably busy, but Mr. Jurillo has been here a long time, and he knows that having teachers in the hallway sometimes prevents problems. One time a parent complained to Mr. Jurillo and wanted her son moved from Corrie's room into my classroom. Corrie and I told Mr. Jurillo that Matt's friends are in my room, so we didn't want the move. We thought he was just bowing under the pressure of the parent. However, he said that the times that he didn't move the child after an extremely adamant parental request, the parent had become overly critical of the teacher during the rest of the year, and everyone suffered. I realized that even though I might not agree with him, Mr. Jurillo usually has a reason behind his decisions. Sometimes he knows more about family situations, sometimes he's had similar experiences, and sometimes he knows more about the underlying problems. I've discovered that he usually tries to treat students and faculty fairly, and I respect that. Yesterday Mr. Jurillo told me that he really likes how you have used group work in teaching fractions. I know that he respects your teaching talents.

By taking an objective stance, mentors can often role model best practices for appreciating others' opinions; by sharing overheard praise, mentors can help new teachers see their own strengths.

✎ · Explaining School Norms and Traditions · ✎

Rob Danin and Margaret Bacon advise that "the culture of a building consists of not only the individuals inside its walls, but also the school's governing norms and procedural structures" (1999, 205). Mentors can help prepare beginning teachers for some of the norms and traditions of a school district or school building, allowing the new teacher to feel acculturated rather than constantly being surprised. For instance, it's helpful for a mentor to explain that the teachers usually stay at school and have pizza delivered prior to a parent/teacher conference evening, that during homecoming a half-day is devoted to float building to provide a student collaborative experience, that the eighth graders are invited to the high school play matinee, that students are often absent on the first day of deer hunting season, or any number of other school oddities that may be peculiar to a particular school or town. Telling the beginning teacher about common jokes around school will help her join in the laughter and be a part of the "inside joke." Mentors need to be attuned to a school culture to help beginning teachers move quickly from being an outsider to an insider.

≫ · Summary · ≫

Mentors can acclimate beginning teachers to the school culture by asking about first impressions of the school, doing a self-analysis of the school culture, providing introductions to faculty and staff, encouraging listening and getting to know colleagues on a personal level, urging participation in staff and committee meetings, and respecting other faculty and colleagues. Just as teachers discover ways to motivate recalcitrant students, so, too, mentors can help new teachers navigate the culture of a particular school and become a viable participant in school decisions.

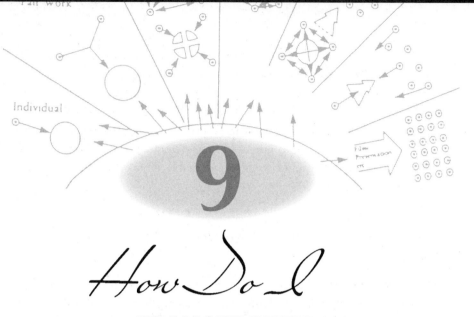

9

How Do I

PROMOTE EFFECTIVE RELATIONSHIPS WITH PARENTS/GUARDIANS?

Christie, an elementary physical education student teacher, watched as her cooperating teacher pulled out a set of note cards as the students lined up at the end of the period. She observed Meridee taking out a pen and beginning to write. "May I ask what you are writing?" Christie asked.

Meridee laughed. "Sure. Each class period I select three students who do something especially good, and I jot a quick note to their parents. Today I'm going to tell Mackenzie's parents that she caught the ball three times today. She is a special education student who has motor coordination problems, so three times is really good for her."

Christie smiled. "How neat! Who else are you going to write to?"

Meridee looked down her list. "I think I'll write to Eduardo's parents about his good teamwork and to Callae's parents about how she helped me put away the equipment. I mark these in my grade book, and I try to send a note to every parent once a semester."

"Wow," Christine exclaimed. "As a phys. ed. teacher, you have hundreds of students. That's a lot of work and record keeping for you."

"Yes, it is," Meridee admitted. "But just watch the kids when I hand them the notes. When I ask, 'Can you take this note to your parents?' they are at first worried, but I let them read the note, and when they see that it's something good, they usually give me a big smile and say, 'Sure, I will. Thanks!' These notes usually get into the parents' hands. Students usually don't lose a note that says something good about them or forget to give it to their parents. In fact, parents sometimes seek me out at parent/teacher conferences to tell me how much they appreciate my two-sentence note."

"I like your idea. Could I write some of the notes?"

Meridee smiled at Christine. "We're going to be a great team."

While much of teacher education is devoted to working with students, perhaps too little focus is given to working with students' first teachers, their parents. Most parent/teacher relationships are quite congenial with parents often volunteering to help chaperone field trips or school dances or by raising money for educational projects through the PTA or other organizations. Collaborating with parents for their children's success can often be highly rewarding, but sometimes a new teacher's first encounters with parents can be a nerve-racking experience. One angry or disgruntled parent can make a school year much more challenging for any teacher, but especially for a beginning teacher. Catherine Brighton writes, "Establishing positive connections between home and school are additional burdens for new teachers. Some parents communicate reticence about dealing with new teachers, fearing that they are largely unorganized, inexperienced, and unable to control student behavior" (1999, 198). Mentors can help beginning teachers recognize how to make interactions with parents an invigorating and mutually beneficial experience for both parents and teachers.

Mentors may wish to devote one or more conferences with the beginning teacher to discussing parent/teacher relationships. It's often helpful to talk about the terminology for a student's guardians. In a typical classroom, students' primary caretakers may include one or more parents, stepparents, grandparents or other relatives, adopted parents, foster parents, international exchange student parents, or other guardians. This wide range of families often causes teachers to wonder about word choices in conversations with students and in letters to caretakers. Mentors can assist beginning teachers in recognizing school policy for which parental figure can take a child home, which guardian(s) receives a report card, who should be contacted in an emergency, or who should be notified or informed about successes or problems. Many schools advocate using an inclusive, singular form of "Dear Parent or Guardian" for a generic newsletter sent to the home. Sometimes, though, this becomes too cumbersome, such as in this chapter, in which, even though we would like to use more inclusive language, we have resorted to the concise, generic term of *parents*. It is important, though, that mentors help beginning teachers to think inclusively.

Beginning teachers often enter teaching with minimal experiences with parents. They may have had discussions and role playing of parent/teacher conferences in teacher education classes, but they often enter teaching with few actual experiences working with parents. In this chapter, we'll discuss how mentors can encourage the beginning teacher's interactions with parents through introductory school activities, parent/teacher conferences, correspondences, and documentation.

❧ · Initial Interactions · ❧

A teacher's initial interactions with parents might be through a newsletter, a website, or a survey. To be proactive and launch the year on a positive note, teachers can send a newsletter home to parents either prior to the first day of school or during the first week of the school year. Whether the letter is written formally or informally, the tone must be professional. Since a beginning teacher often wonders how deeply to describe the curriculum, as well as how much to reveal about personal life, mentors can show sample letters from various faculty members and volunteer to read and comment on the letter if the beginning teacher desires. By perusing the letter, the mentor can point out the letter's positive traits, as well as possible misconstrued or omitted information, or even mechanical errors such as misspellings. Of course, if the beginning teacher doesn't wish to have you, as the mentor, preview the letter, then graciously accept this decision, recognizing either the teacher's level of confidence or desire for independence.

In today's technological world, it's also helpful to have a teacher's website in which an introductory letter to parents can be included. While many beginning teachers may be more technologically astute than their mentors, usually the launch of a school year is too hectic for new teachers to develop their own websites. It's often helpful for mentors to show beginning teachers how to use generic software or to suggest a technology person to help create a teacher's website. Either way it's important to keep the website simple and concise so a new teacher can devote time to setting up the classroom and developing lesson plans.

While the newsletter and website are one-way communicative vehicles, some teachers use surveys to make the communication interactive. Barb LeClaire (2006), who teaches second grade at White Bear Lake in Minneapolis, encourages sending home a parent/guardian survey, such as the following, to get to know parents and to extend a positive message of support and partnership in helping students succeed:

Parent/Guardian Survey

1. What are the greatest strengths of your child that you would like me to encourage?

2. What are areas of difficulty that your child has experienced that you would like me to work on?

3. What are concerns that your child has about school?

4. What are your hopes and dreams for your child?

5. What is the most important thing that you want your child to learn in ___ grade?

6. How can I best serve your child?

If the survey is not returned, mentors can encourage beginning teachers to continue sending surveys home. If the third survey is not returned, the teacher can write in red marker "Please read. Important." If the surveys are still not returned, the teacher can call the parent to establish an initial, positive two-way communication.

Some grade-level or interdisciplinary teams may wish to compose a newsletter, website, or survey together. This reduces the time required by the beginning teacher to produce new communication pieces while encouraging the new teacher's input.

Open Houses and Parent/Teacher Conferences

Newsletters, websites, and surveys are helpful, but face-to-face meetings serve as perhaps the most important communication venues. These might take the form of open houses, back-to-school nights, or parent/teacher conferences.

Many schools host an open house for parents/guardians during the first weeks of school. Jim Burke (2007) recommends preparing a handout, displaying student work, wearing professional attire, greeting parents upon their entrance, and emphasizing teacher availability for future conferences or email exchanges. He also gives parents index cards with questions similar to the survey questions suggested earlier. Mentors can help prepare beginning teachers for these occasions by describing the general procedures: who greets parents upon entering the building, how long parents usually stay in the classroom, whether teachers are expected to talk to the parents as a group or individually, what displays are usually provided, how many parents to expect, and where refreshments or other information (book fairs, etc.) are located. Beginning teachers will often feel more comfortable with a routine: greeting parents, introducing themselves, saying something positive about the student, giving a handout or index card, and inviting parents to circulate around the room. Mentors might role play situations with beginning teachers to help them feel more comfortable in this new situation.

Middle schools and high schools sometimes sponsor a back-to-school night in which parents adopt their child's schedule and move from classroom to classroom, hearing a summary of each class for ten to fifteen minutes. Mentors and beginning teachers can jointly rehearse their own description of the course. Beginning teachers, who are often technologically adept, may wish to present a PowerPoint presentation, keeping the presentation organized and allowing the parents' eyes to be directed to the screen rather than directly to the speaker. Since the session usually concludes with a question-and-answer time, mentors can help prepare beginning teachers with typical parental questions.

Of course, the most common encounter with parents is the parent/teacher conference. While beginning teachers are often acquainted with various school procedures in their past observational role as a student, they probably have not directly experienced parent/teacher conferences unless they themselves have children. Ellen Moir states,

> Parent conferences require new teachers to be highly organized, articulate, tactful, and prepared to confer with parents about each student's progress. This type of communication with parents can be awkward and difficult for beginning teachers. New teachers generally begin with the idea that parents are partners in the learning process, and they are not prepared for parents' concerns or criticisms. (1999, 21)

To assist new teachers in preparing for conferences, mentors can discuss the procedures and rehearse various encounters. Some teachers prepare folders with student work and use the time to explain the curriculum and show the student's strengths and weaknesses (or "areas to work toward") in the particular subject area. Other teachers create note cards with specific comments tailored to each student, allowing them to use the sandwich technique: saying something positive, presenting the student's difficulties or challenges with the work, and concluding with ways the parents and teacher can work together for positive results. Yet others like to begin on a conversational note of talking about the student's interests prior to talking about the student's academic work.

Mentors working with student teachers might model the first conferences, then invite the student teacher to give added comments, and gradually move toward having the student teacher takes a leadership role in the conference. In a middle school or high school situation in which the student teacher is teaching various classes and the cooperating teacher has not yet turned over other classes, the student teacher can take a leadership role in the conferences with the parents of the students she is currently teaching. This initial experience will help the beginner feel more confident in future parent/teacher conferences.

Mentors can help make beginning teachers aware of the concerns that parents bring with them. Sidney Trubowitz and Maureen Picard Robins refer to "parents who themselves experienced schools as places of failure, parents whose family life is in disarray, parents with unrealistic expectations for their children, and parents whose cultural values are out of sync with those of the school" (2003, 80). Other parents may seem quiet-natured and remain silent during the conference, may be non-English speakers who require a translator, or may have little or no control over their children and frankly admit their deficiencies. For instance, a beginning teacher may be excited to see a parent at a parent/teacher conference in which a student has earned an A– in class, thinking that this will be an easy conference to negotiate, only to discover that the parent is angry that the student doesn't have an A on the report card.

Veteran teachers will often remark that each conference time often contains a new surprise, so mentors might prepare beginning teachers that occasionally a parent may cry, become angry, or seem apathetic. Sometimes a parent takes a negative comment personally, presuming that if a child is not doing well, it must be the parent's fault. Mentors can show how to reassure parents by discussing or role playing possible encounters, illustrating how to defuse a problematic situation. While this might make some beginning teachers even more nervous, usually new teachers prefer to feel prepared, even for unlikely events.

Mentors need to emphasize that just as classes need to be learner centered, so, too, parent/teacher conferences should be parent centered. Teachers can encourage parents to describe their child's interests and goals, to ask questions, and to share their concerns. Questions such as "What would you like me to know about your son?" or "What questions would you like to ask about your daughter's work?" might lead to fruitful conversations. Most important, though, is for teachers to ask, "What ideas do you have for how we can help your child improve as a student? How can we work toward this goal together?" To create a true parent/teacher partnership, the conference needs to conclude with a two-way action plan: for instance, with the parent providing a work space and specified time for homework and the teacher agreeing to inform the parent of progress or problems with homework completion. Mentors can help beginning teachers realize that what they say during a conference is often less important than what they ask and how well they listen.

Many schools have moved toward a student-led parent/teacher conference, which may not have been the beginning teacher's experience in his own school years, his practicum, or his student teaching. In this instance, it's helpful for mentors to explain the procedure and to prepare students to become leaders in the conference. If these conferences are interdisciplinary, the beginning teacher may not see some of the parents of her own students, so she may want to set up individual conferences at another time for parents of struggling students.

In the following conversation, interdisciplinary team members describe to their new colleague how they prepare for parent/teacher conferences:

Amanda: *Since parent-teacher conferences are scheduled for next week, let's talk about what we can do to prepare. For instance, Kevin, since you're a new teacher, you might have questions for us.*

Kevin: *Well I'd like to hear you describe a typical conference and what I should do to prepare.*

Betty: *What were you planning to do to prepare?*

Kevin: *Frankly, I hadn't thought about it. I just figured I'd answer the parents' questions.*

Betty: *Well, the most common question is, "How is my son or daughter doing in your class?" How can you prepare for that question?*

Kevin: *I guess I should have my grade book with me so I can look up the grades and assignment completions.*

Sam: *That's helpful. Sometimes I make a note card for each student with one positive comment and one goal for improvement.*

Kevin: *Um, I could try that.*

Amanda: *Would you like to see us role play some conferences?*

Kevin: *That would be great!*

Amanda: *If we each role played being the teacher, Kevin could see our different conference styles, and then he could decide which way suits him.*

Kevin: *Super! Could you role play a typical conference and then some difficult ones, such as a student not doing the work or a student who is the class clown? Then maybe I could role play the teacher's role and get in some practice.*

Amanda: *OK, let's try it.*

Sam: *Let's go for it!*

Helping beginning teachers know what to expect during conferences will assist them in feeling more prepared and confident as they initiate parent/teacher partnerships.

✐ · Unexpected Conferences · ✐

Open houses, back-to-school nights, and parent/teacher conferences, are planned occasions. Often the most demanding experience for the beginning teacher is the unexpected conference, as in the example below:

Maddy burst into Deanna's room with a stricken face. "What's wrong?" Deanna asked.

"Mr. Muir just told me that Bob Wiler's mom is coming in to see me after school. She thinks her son should have gotten a higher grade."

Deanna motioned Maddy to sit down and asked, "So how do you think you should handle the conference?"

"I don't know."

"Will Mr. Muir be present?"

"Gosh, I didn't ask."

"Is Bob going to be there with his mom?"

"I don't know that either."

"Is Mrs. Wiler concerned about one grade or an overall grade?"

"I don't have any idea. Maybe I should see if Mr. Muir knows more about the situation."

"Yes, that would be helpful. How will you start the conference?"

"I guess I'll ask Mrs. Wiler to tell me what she's concerned about? Would that be OK?"

"That's a good start. Instead of seeing this negatively as meeting with an upset parent, maybe you can view it positively as a parent who genuinely cares about her son."

"You're right. Maybe I'll start by thanking her for coming and for taking an interest in her son's work at school."

"I like that idea. Now how can you prepare for this conference? Do you have any of Bob's work or a record of his grades that you can share with Mrs. Wiler?"

"That's good. That would make me look prepared and give me something concrete to discuss. Thanks, Deanna!"

While questioning and role playing are often a mentor's best tools, sometimes immediate situations call for helping the beginning teacher adopt a positive tone, initiate the conversation, and prepare artifacts. Other sudden parent situations may arise with emails or phone calls, such as in the following situation:

In checking her email during her planning period, Carolyn discovered a message from the father of one of her second-grade students, in which he berated her for letting a fifth-grade student bully his son at lunch and destroy his son's lunchbox. The email asked, "What kind of school is this? Don't you supervise the children? Why did you allow a bullying situation like this?"

Carolyn was immediately upset about the tone of the email, which appeared to blame her for a situation about which she was totally unaware. She immediately printed the email and went next door to talk to her mentor, Barb, who was seated at a table at the back of the room, reading student writings.

Waving the email aloft, Carolyn told Barb, "This is unbelievable. I got an email from an irate father who is blaming me for a situation that I know nothing about."

Barb motioned to Carolyn to be seated at the table, and she silently read the email. "Hmmm. He says that a fifth grader destroyed Jimmy's lunchbox yesterday during lunch. Since the second graders and fifth graders eat in two different sections of the lunchroom, that seems rather unlikely."

"Yeah, I didn't think of that. I was so mad, I guess I didn't read the email carefully. Should I email the father and tell him that would be impossible?"

"Sometimes it's helpful to have all the facts before talking to parents. Have you met Jimmy's father? What is he like?"

"No, I don't know him. He didn't come to our open house, and Jimmy rides the bus, so his father has never come into my room."

"How do you think you could find out more information about this situation?"

"Well, I could talk to Jimmy or I could talk to those who are sitting near him at lunch."

"That's a good idea!"

"When the students come back from music, we're going to have free reading time, so I'll start by talking to Abhe who sits next to Jimmy at lunch. Is there anything else I should do?"

"Yes, you might fill Mrs. Minniken in on the situation. Sometimes the next step is for the parent to call the principal, so it might be wise to tell her about the situation."

"OK, thanks, Barb."

After school that day, Carolyn told Barb that when she had asked Abhe if he knew anything about Jimmy's lunchbox, he said, "Uh-huh." When pressed to tell more, he said, "Jimmy wrecked the lunchbox himself, but it was an accident. His father had just bought it for him and had told him to take care of it, so he told me he was afraid to tell his father."

Carolyn sent Abhe back in the room and whispered for Jimmy to come talk to her in the hallway. "I received an email today from your father, and he seemed pretty upset about your lunchbox."

Jimmy lowered his head and nodded.

"Well, I don't know anything about your lunchbox. What happened?"

Jimmy bit his lip. "It got destroyed."

"And how did that happen?"

"I grabbed the side of it instead of the handles like I was supposed to and the side got torn. I was so angry that my new plastic lunchbox was torn that I just ripped off the whole side. It had Superman on it."

"And then your dad saw it?" Carolyn prompted.

"Yeah. He was really mad because he told me to take care of it."

"What did you tell your dad?"

Jimmy looked at the floor. "I said a fifth-grade bully took it away from me at lunchtime and tore it."

"Thank you for telling me what really happened. You know I'm going to have to tell your dad what really happened."

"Uh-huh, I know. I'll get grounded."

Carolyn told Barb that she had emailed the father, explaining the situation. She waved the second email. "Here's his response: 'OK, that's what I figured had happened.' Look at that! He didn't even apologize for blaming me."

Barb laughed. "Well, some parents are like that, but most parents are more considerate. He just wanted you to check on what happened, and you did."

Carolyn huffed, "Well, he could have asked me about it rather than blaming me!"

Barb smiled again. "I know. Let's look at what you can take away from this situation. What did you learn that you can use for future parent encounters?"

After thinking for a moment, Carolyn answered, "Well, I learned that it's helpful if I wait before responding. That way the parent can cool down, and I can, too!"

"Right! Anything else?"

"I learned that it's always wise to check out the facts before responding to a parent and that I should always inform the principal. Mrs. Minniken was really supportive when I told her first about the email and later what had happened."

✍ · Technology Aids · ✍

Parent and teacher groups have been longtime advocates of parental involvement within the school. Technology has aided that involvement while sometimes providing an additional expectation and higher stress level for teachers. Mentors can help beginning teachers balance the ideal versus real expectations.

Email, as shown in Carolyn's encounter, allows teachers and parents to have immediate and direct access to each other, especially when both parents are working and aren't easily accessible by phone. While email allows quick reports to parents and is often a more direct route to parents than a note sent through the child, care needs to be taken to assure that the proper tone is conveyed to parents, so the message is not misinterpreted. In challenging situations, a mentor can question a beginning teacher about the pros and cons of each medium—email, phone call, or note sent home—and help the beginning teacher arrive at a practical decision. In the past, a teacher's preparation time could often be solely devoted to preparing materials or responding to papers, but today many teachers spend part or all of a class period responding to parental questions or concerns, as shown by this example:

Mitchell, a middle school teacher, hurriedly wrote the following email to Dijon's parents: "Dijon didn't turn in his social studies homework again today." He was ready to press "Send" and then decided that maybe more information would be helpful. After talking to his mentor after school, he realized that Dijon's parents might read the message as, "Why didn't you make sure that Dijon did his homework?" A longer message, while requiring more teacher time, often provides a more collaborative tone. After some thought, Mitchell revised the message in this way:

"I enjoyed meeting you at last week's parent/teacher conference, and I appreciate your wish to be informed when Dijon does not complete his homework. While

Dijon did complete yesterday's homework, he has not yet started his research on a country for social studies even though students were to have located their first three resources by today. I asked Dijon about his areas of interest, and he told me that he wanted to research Peru since his aunt had traveled there. I helped Dijon locate some introductory resources. Would it be possible for Dijon to contact his aunt to interview her or get materials from her? Perhaps together you and I can encourage Dijon to begin working on this larger, long-range assignment. If you have questions about this project, you or Dijon might check the directions that are located on my teacher website. Also, feel free to email me with your questions. Thanks for working with me to encourage Dijon on this assignment."

By electing to compose a longer email, Mitchell established a friendlier, more informative message, which invited the parents' collaboration. Perhaps by working as a team, Mitchell and Dijon's parents can encourage Dijon to use his talents to create a successful learning experience.

Technology has also provided opportunities for teachers to communicate assignments and grades. Just as Mitchell provided a teacher website with the directions and due date for each part of a research project, so, too, teachers can keep parents informed about the exciting things happening in the classroom. A teacher's website not only allows instructors to inform students and parents about "what" is being taught, but it can also provide an opportunity to explain "why" the assignment is important. Again, explaining "why" requires additional teacher time, but mentors can show beginning teachers effective websites and explain the relevance of the subject matter. Since beginning teachers often have more technological experience, they might become team leaders in creating these effective sites.

The technological age also provides new means of communicating student grades. Many schools now use a grading program that allows students and parents to view a secure site to see the student's progress in completing assignments and earning grades. Of course, such sites require more teacher time to update the continually changing information. This adds one more burden to overtaxed teachers since students and parents often expect quick turnaround in grading. While immediate postings may be possible for multiple-choice tests, teachers need more time to assess and post essay tests, compositions, or research projects. Often mentors can help beginning teachers to place a disclaimer on the website stating the need for more time for these lengthier assessments.

Of course, all of these technology uses raise the question of parental access since not all parents may have funds for computers or Internet use or have time to access information at a library. Teachers also need to consider how to provide this information to those who do not use computers or who lack ready access.

✎ · Communication Logs and Documentation · ✎

Many teachers maintain a communication log with parents. Usually the parents and teacher record notes about the child's behavior so that all parties can be aware of the situation. This especially works well for parents who have children with attention-deficit hyperactive disorder (ADHD) and want to give medical personnel a record of behaviors prior to medication or record behaviors while on medication.

Sometimes parents going through a divorce or separation want a behavior or emotional log in which the teacher records behaviors so the parents are aware of the stress the child may be undergoing (and the parents record behaviors in a similar fashion). For instance, the teacher might record the type of day the student experienced, if the student seemed sad, shared his or her feelings, or had trouble staying focused on schoolwork. For instance, the teacher might record if he or she gave the student a time-out or if the student asked to see the counselor.

Similarly, the parent records whether the child was silent, talkative, or acted in unusual ways at home. If the student has a good day, the teacher might include a smiley-face sticker; if the student has a challenging day, the teacher might write the facts with an honest rejoinder such as "Hopefully, tomorrow will be better for Peter."

Other times, the communication log may be used to record assignments, due and completed. This might help students who are not task oriented or are struggling with emotional problems and cannot concentrate on schoolwork. Sometimes parents prefer that the child carry the communication log, others prefer email correspondence, and yet others want a communication log or assignment notebook sent to each parent. Teachers need to ask whether parents want one file to be shared or a double file to be sent separately (e.g., a "Mom" folder and a "Dad" folder). It's important for both parent(s) and teacher to follow through by maintaining the ongoing correspondence.

Mentors can also help beginning teachers form a type of documentation for behaviors. Whether recorded on note cards, in a day planner, or on a computer file, teachers can list the date and the specific behavior so they can see whether patterns develop. This documentation may be helpful during team meetings or parent conferences.

✎ · Summary · ✎

Mentors can help beginning teachers create positive parent/teacher relationships by encouraging the following:

- Preparing a newsletter or teacher website

- Getting to know the parents through surveys, open houses, and conferences

- Role playing various parent scenarios prior to conferences

- Obtaining as much information as possible before contacting the parents

- Waiting a few hours before responding to an irate phone or email message, thereby allowing a "cool down time" for both parent and teacher

- Informing administrators about situations in case the parent decides to contact higher personnel

- Working with an academic team to provide cohesive communication across subject areas

- Sending positive notes when students perform well

- Using technology as an aid to immediate, positive correspondence or to displaying homework requirements or course grades

- Documenting students' behaviors either through a joint communication log shared with parents or in a confidential print or electronic file

By helping the beginning teacher establish positive parent relationships, mentors can assist the new teacher in having a more productive year and perhaps remaining longer in the teaching profession. Mentors can help beginning teachers experience the joys of working with parents and envision new ways of forming effective parent partnerships.

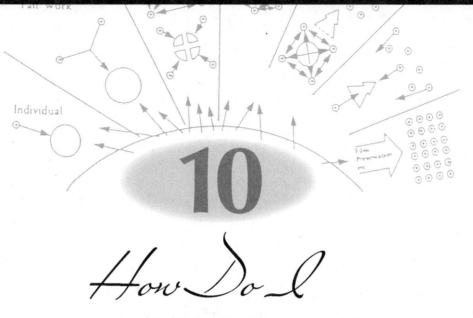

Individual

How Do I

PROVIDE MENTORING OPPORTUNITIES DURING CURRICULUM MAPPING?

"So, Carmen, what do you know about the middle school curriculum here at La Costa?" Marge, the district curriculum director, asked of new teacher Carmen Vasquez.

"Well, I feel like I'm getting a handle on the language arts curriculum," Carmen responded.

"Well, that's necessary, of course, but I'm talking more of the larger curriculum of the school, how language arts fits into math and social studies and science. And then, I'd like us to take it a step further and focus on how the seventh-grade curriculum prepares the eighth-grade and how those in turn, prepare the ninth-grade curriculum," said Marge.

"Wow. No, I don't have a good sense of that. And curriculum mapping is not something we discussed a great deal at the university, except to be aware that it exists and that a lot of districts are using curriculum mapping to give teachers the big picture."

"That's what I thought. But don't look so worried. Your mentor, Carolina, and I will use this as another opportunity to mentor you and the other new teachers here at La Costa into both the school and the curriculum," said Marge with a smile.

As schools look toward ways to promote collegial conversations among their educators, many principals and superintendents have focused on curriculum mapping as the means of accomplishing their goals. According to Heidi Hayes Jacobs,

> Curriculum mapping is a procedure for collecting data about the operational curriculum in a school and in a district—the instruction that students are experiencing. By mapping what's actually taught and when it's taught, teachers produce data that they can use in conjunction with assessment data to make cumulative revisions in instruction. (Perkins-Gough 2003, 12)

This chapter will deal specifically with the following:

1. Why curriculum mapping has become such a popular means of responding to curriculum reform or revision in school districts.

2. How curriculum mapping can provide mentoring opportunities that support beginning teachers who often find themselves in schools where clear lines of communication among areas and grade levels are not present, making it difficult for them to understand why they're being asked to teach what they teach.

3. How curriculum mapping can be used as a type of mentoring support for all teachers in a district.

✍ · What Is Curriculum Mapping? · ✍

As noted earlier, curriculum mapping, typically created in a dynamic electronic format, allows teachers and districts to collect data both horizontally (across subject areas) and vertically (across grade levels) in order to examine what students are actually learning and how that aligns with district, state, and national educational goals. The basic concept of the vertical mapping is to allow all teachers within a discipline to look at the various local and state assessments for which they are responsible and consider how they are meeting these. For example, middle school language arts teachers can, at each grade level, match their individual curriculums to state standards in the discipline. Then the teachers discuss how the yearly curricula are meeting standards, where the curricula overlap, and how they, as middle school teachers, will address this overlap. This approach creates conversations with elementary language arts and high school English teachers within the school district, creating an optimal sense of how the entire curriculum is supporting student intellectual growth.

Horizontal mapping also encourages teachers within a school site to discuss curriculum with their counterparts in all disciplines. This type of reporting allows teachers to consider how, for example, writing is being addressed across the curriculum by a number of teachers/ disciplines or how a number of educators may be addressing critical thinking throughout their content areas to support a larger school goal or a state assessment. Further, it provides an opportunity for colleagues to talk across disciplines, an activity that is rarely accomplished in most schools.

School districts tend to turn to curriculum mapping when principals or curriculum directors note teacher talk that seems at cross-purposes to curricular goals or when they must meet statewide assessments and content standards but have not developed curricular evaluation tools. The move to mapping can be controversial if the school administration doesn't clearly identify why future preparation and inservice time will be spent on a closer consideration of a school's overall curriculum. Botched communications can leave teachers wondering whether upper administrators are questioning their instructional techniques, classroom pedagogy, or professionalism. Further, some administrators have instituted curriculum mapping without giving their teachers adequate time or technology to sustain their efforts.

Since this chapter will focus on mentoring using curriculum mapping, we will address this approach with a best-case scenario and show how it can be effective for mentors and administrators who want to help their new faculty understand the "big picture" in terms of district and school curriculum. Additional information about curriculum mapping is available at the websites listed in Resources for Teachers.

✍ · Mentoring Using Horizontal Curriculum Mapping · ✍

"Let me introduce Dr. Ron Kellogg. He's a professor in English Education from Northern State University and he's going to work with you as you work on and discuss your curriculum mapping today," said Marge to the language arts teachers from La Costa Middle School.

"It's great to be here. Call me Ron. I'd like to start by going around the room and having each of you tell me who you are and the grade level you teach."

> After the introductions were complete, Ron asked the teachers to take out the resources they had brought with them to help them start the mapping. Some of the veteran teachers pulled out year-long syllabi; newer educators opened up manila files with unit syllabi. "Okay, let's start by having each of you work with the other teachers from your grade area and discuss what is supposed to be covered in terms of content over the course of the year. Each group needs to take a sheet of butcher paper . . . "

For most school sites, encouraging teachers to work with colleagues in their own discipline is typically the best way to initiate curriculum mapping. For new educators in the building, working with veteran teachers who have taught that same curriculum is a huge benefit and provides both groups of teachers with an informal opportunity to ask questions and share ideas.

Discipline-Specific Mentoring

The concept of discipline-specific mentors provides the potential for strong mentor-beginning teacher relationships for many reasons. Discipline-specific mentors are, essentially, content experts who have experience teaching a specific course over time. They have already made necessary adjustments to their curricula, typically in light of school goals or changes in the mission or to adopt content standards as encouraged by their professional organizations or mandated by initiatives such as No Child Left Behind. Finally, they have weathered various class/student personalities and have created adaptations of various activities that they can share with less-experienced counterparts.

Further, in the introductory example, we see an administration not only willing to set up mentoring for its beginning teachers but also inclined to support its veteran teachers through what Jane Rankin, a director of curriculum for the College Station Independent School District in College Station, Texas, has termed a "curriculum coach": "a facilitator . . . called a curriculum coach. I meet regularly with the coaches . . . they come up with ways for teachers to collaborate at the grade level and the timeline for collaboration" (Rankin 2003, 1).

The curriculum coach can be either someone from the district who is a known entity to the teachers or an outside associate—like Ron Kellogg from our example—who brings in content expertise and, possibly, a more neutral view of how to look at curriculum. Also, since we're being honest, teachers are often more comfortable with an outside support person who doesn't have a direct link to administration. In either case, the curriculum coach must have a record of solid teaching experience in the content area; thorough knowledge of state and national standards, benchmarks, and assessments; and the ability to direct and support teachers as they develop and analyze their curriculum maps. In addition, the coach must also be available during the many inservices in which the teachers will be working, both to serve as a sounding board for ideas and to offer suggestions as necessary.

Mentoring the Mapping

The North Central Regional Educational Lab (2003, 2) suggests the following steps for initial curriculum mapping within a subject area:

1. Identify major units
2. Add concepts and topics
3. Add skills
4. Validate
5. Map the standards and benchmarks

This section will discuss each in some detail and then delineate how mentors can use these steps in supporting mentees.

Identify Major Units. In this first step, teachers will individually or together determine the major units or themes of a course. Veteran teachers can clearly take the lead in describing the course content. By using large sheets of butcher paper, each grade level can show the course content and sequence to other content-area teachers, as well as new teachers.

Add Concepts and Topics. During the second phase of the mapping, the teacher team adds to the butcher paper (or computer) the topics and concepts taught by unit or during a specific time in the curriculum. Again, mentors can discuss the timing and scaffolding of certain topics or concepts.

Add Skills. This step may be one of the most important mentoring opportunities since beginning teachers are more aware of concepts than they are of the skills necessary to help students internalize concepts. Mentor/mentee conversations in this area can also support beginning teachers as they consider logical connections between skills and concepts and ways to build the knowledge base for both students and early-career teachers.

Validate. During the validation phase, which can last anywhere from a week to a month, depending on the next meeting date, teachers can return to the map with additional ideas or thoughts.

Map the Standards and Benchmarks. During the final phase, content teachers connect the concepts, issues, and skills noted on the map with the appropriate state or national standards and local benchmarks. Again, mentors can reiterate the connection of standards and benchmarks to student learning and curriculum development. Also, this may be a prime opportunity for the curriculum coach to share additional ideas or suggestions about how broadly the standards/benchmarks can be defined. In this way, the curriculum coach can mentor the mentors and provide much-valued professional development opportunities without additional cost or travel.

> Carmen took another look at the curriculum map she and her fellow seventh-grade language arts teachers had recently completed and verified. While the map was full of information about units, topics, and skills, Carmen was still a bit puzzled as to what she was going to learn from the map. After all, at this point in the semester, she had only taught two three-week units and had touched on a small number of the topics and skills discussed in the earliest pieces of the map. The assessments she had made of her students' work so far had been a mixed bag, with one in particular making her aware that she would need to spend more time crafting end-of-unit tests.
>
> At that moment, Carmen's mentor, Carolina, came into the room. "You ready to make sense of this map in terms of assessment?" Carolina said with a smile.
>
> "Absolutely. And I'm so glad that we can do this together. I'd never admit it to Marge, but I'm not totally clear on what she wants us to focus on for this. I mean, I think I'm starting to see what I'm doing well and not so well in assessing my students, but I'm not sure how to take this and make connections to the state test."
>
> "I think we'll stick with our local assessments to begin with and go from there. Why don't you tell me about the kinds of assessments you've used in the units you've taught so far. Then I'll walk you through a critical inquiry approach that will allow us to evaluate your assessments in connection to the standards."
>
> "Ok. Well, we can start here with the pretest I gave them on Day 2 so that I would have a better sense of their ability to write basic paragraphs."

Once the basic mapping has been completed and colleagues have had an opportunity to discuss "what and how they enact units and assessments," mentors or curriculum coaches can engage the group in an examination of what needs improvement in the curriculum, how to make those improvements, and who should be the leaders. When working with new teachers at the school site or younger educators generally, mentors may need to describe the various standardized tests used by the district/state to assess student learning and discuss what that has looked like historically at the school. This should provide the mentors with excellent talking points to present the types of activities/assessments that have provided strong data in the past and help the mentees create activities and approaches based on best practices. Mentors can also talk about what they're learning about their own assessments through the mapping activity. For example:

> "I've noticed," said Carolina, "that my students make a lot of forward movement on their writing until we get to the persuasive essay, and I've been looking over what I do with that paper that seems to stall them. Up to that point, they seem to be getting topic sentences, but when I teach the thesis statement in conjunction with attention-getting ways to get the reader involved in their topic, I notice that they have problems. So I think I'm going to need to break those two items apart more clearly so that they have mastery, or at least as much as eighth graders can have that, over one concept before they move on to the next. And we do need to make sure that students understand this because the last two writing prompts on the state test have required persuasive essays. I've been playing with the idea of having students work on the attention-getters first because honestly, I run into college students who still don't have complete mastery over thesis statements. But then I think, well, maybe if I spent more time on those thesis statements…. What do you think, Carmen?"

This type of critical inquiry allows the mentor to model good practice in determining how effectively curricula is being developed and administered with students. Carolina notes what is working (process writing) as well as trouble spots she has noted in the past (development of thesis statements in opening paragraphs). In her discussion of mastery issues, she provides an example of what she has noticed generally, then uses that as a means of moving the conversation into her mentee's corner so that Carmen can comment on what Carolina has done and offer her own insights. This approach also allows the mentee to ask questions about specific methods the mentor has tried that have or have not been entirely successful, especially in conjunction with standardized testing and other state tests and may allow both to work toward a new understanding of teaching concepts that enhance student learning.

A further step in curriculum map mentoring occurs when teachers across grade levels sit down to discuss where there is overlap in content.

> Carman and Carolina met with their colleagues at the seventh- and ninth-grade levels to discuss concepts and standards that all three grades had to share.

⊱ · Summary · ⊰

While many of us go into teaching because we want the joy of teaching some aspect of our content, we also come to the realization that we are responsible for a variety of subject matter that is important to our students for many different reasons. Standards, assessments, and student outcomes are clearly driving curricula in this country, and educators at all levels need to embrace this reality and make it work for them and their students.

Curriculum mapping is not only an approach that has become very popular with administrators but also one that can accomplish a needed overview of a content or district curriculum if done well. The mentoring that can result from a review of curriculum can support the work already being done by mentors and mentees and provide an inexperienced teacher with additional mentoring above and beyond what has been offered by the assigned mentor.

11

How Should

MENTORS COMMUNICATE WITH ADMINISTRATORS?

Capacity is generated through relationships.

—Anonymous

Perhaps the relationship between the mentor and building administrators is one of the trickiest and most delicately balanced of those to develop and maintain. Mentors are generally practicing teachers or teachers on special assignment, and they generally do not hold administrative credentials. Mentors and administrators frequently share the same fundamental goals of improving instruction and increasing student learning. Both mentors and administrators work with new or developing teachers who struggle with classroom management or with instructional techniques. It could be that both mentors and building administrators observe and work with the same colleague—even on the same day, perhaps.

Mentors and building administrators assume different roles: building administrators play a contractual, evaluative role, and mentors do not. Thus it is critical that mentors and building administrators understand their differing roles and responsibilities. Without clear guidance in terms of roles and responsibilities, the lines between mentor and evaluator may blur and create a stressful environment for new colleague and mentor alike.

⤙ · Roles and Boundaries · ⤚

One of the most important tasks of an administrator is to hire and then evaluate teachers in the school. Most principals want to provide helpful feedback to colleagues new to the school or who might be working on pedagogical skills, but they temper enthusiasm with the knowledge that sometimes performance evaluations cannot be positive and may lead to disciplinary action. School contracts generally require that administrators visit classrooms and evaluate teachers on an annual or biannual basis. Administrators are also responsible for overseeing and, if needed, disciplining teachers and for placing less-than-capable teachers on plans of improvement that may, in the end, lead to termination.

The mentor's role differs considerably in terms of responsibilities. While the administrator is bound by the school district's contract with all of the evaluation criteria, the mentor should be concerned with improving instruction and developing solid, collegial relationships. The mentor's roles will certainly evolve with time, but clarity from the beginning helps define guidelines and limits that make for productive relationships.

Consider Laura's comments on the importance of determining roles for administrators and mentors. In her third year as mentor in an elementary school setting, Laura reflects on what she has learned about determining roles and responsibilities in the mentoring/administrator relationship.

> Trust is the big thing. Lose it and then all is lost. On the one hand, you have to develop trust with the person you are mentoring, and then with the building principal as well. So it is terribly important for everyone in the relationship—and it is a relationship—to understand their roles and then the lines between coaching to improve teaching and the kinds of evaluation regularly conducted by a principal.

What is critical when defining roles is to establish the mentor as a nonevaluator—a person whose sole purpose is to support, enhance, and encourage new colleagues to improve and thrive in a school setting. This is not to say that mentors will not *evaluate* what they are seeing in terms of quality and then suggest ways to improve instruction. Such analysis happens regularly in the mentoring relationship. Successful mentors, however, must establish an identity, and with the help of the administrator, perhaps in the first faculty meeting, the mentor's role can be set as a clear, nonevaluative one.

Mentors may use the language in the evaluation tool (e.g., student engagement, planning, checking for understanding) but must be mindful that their conversations should not "sound" evaluative. Clearly articulating the responsibilities of the principal and mentor to the beginning teacher helps to begin a trusting relationship that can lead to improved instruction. As one veteran mentor comments, "Mentors need to consistently remind all stakeholders of their nonadmin position, even as they find synthesis with the administrative staff."

❧ · Communication with Established Guidelines · ❧

Strong communication helps to develop strong and lasting relationships among all stakeholders. As we noted earlier, clear roles for mentors and principals—roles that set them apart in terms of responsibilities—help to develop productive relationships. The development of a communication plan between mentor and building administrators is equally as important as determining their separate roles.

Kami, an elementary principal of five years, commented on her initial questions about how to interact with a mentor:

> I wasn't sure how to begin with the mentor. OK, I've got a mentor in my building working with new teachers, and then I am responsible for getting in the teachers' classrooms to evaluate them for instruction. So at first I wondered, how do we work this? I mean, what should the relationship between the mentor and the principal look like? I understood the relationship between the mentor and the new kid on the block. That was clear. But how should I interact with the mentor and teacher? So I set a meeting in hopes of developing ground rules. I felt that we needed ground rules.

With little experience working with a mentor, Kami's intuitive sense of setting ground rules in a relationship helped her to determine appropriate lines of communication. We recommend that such meetings between building principals and mentors take place early, before the beginning of the school year, and that they be held several times during the school year to keep communication flowing in positive directions.

Critical to this is for all parties to avoid "communication triangles" where the mentor becomes the conduit for information from the building administrator to the beginning teacher or vice versa. To avoid the "triangle," mentors need to speak directly to teachers with whom they are working, and they must make sure that principals know that if they have something to communicate to teachers being mentored, they must speak directly to the teacher without using the mentor as a filter, buffer, or reinforcement. Mentors also want to encourage teachers with whom they are working to speak directly to the principal about concerns they have about a building administrator's policies, comments, or evaluations. In other words, in most cases mentors want to encourage direct, face-to-face conversations whenever possible.

A seasoned veteran teacher and a mentor assigned to several buildings in her school district, Karen experienced a situation all too frequent in the mentor-principal relationship. She expressed her frustration with a principal who went "fishing" in a hallway conversation:

> My background is math, and I was working with a beginning middle school math teacher when one of the assistant principals stopped me in the hall and said that he was just in a teacher's classroom. I was working with the teacher. And the assistant principal wanted to know what I thought about the teacher's performance. First of all, I didn't appreciate the place where we had this conversation, and then I felt as though the administrator was fishing for something. I don't like it when they fish. There is a code of confidentiality that must be maintained, so I turned it back on the assistant principal and asked him what he was noticing. Boy, I did not feel good about that conversation at all.

Many mentors share Karen's frustrations with being placed in difficult conversations that in the end will create communication triangles that may violate trust and that complicate productive working relationships. Karen employed the strategy of turning the comment back to the person who posed the question. This helped to protect confidentiality while respectfully continuing the conversation with the building administrator. Mentors like Karen face these tough questions continually and have recommended the following choices of boilerplate responses or guides when responding.

Following an Administrator's Positive Statement

- "It sounds like you are happy that _____ is a member of the school's faculty. Will you share that with him?"

- "Thank you for sharing that with me. You seem to appreciate what _____ is doing in her classroom."

Following an Administrator's Inquiry or Question

- "It sounds as though you are curious to know about _____'s performance. I wish that I could share more, but I cannot. I would be happy to listen."

- "I wish that I could say more here, but the mentoring relationship is confidential. Will you ask _____ that question personally?"

Following an Administrator's Negative Comment

- "I sense that you want to share your frustration about what you are feeling, but I cannot talk with you about this because the mentoring relationship is confidential."

- "It sounds as if you have concerns about _____'s teaching performance. Can you share them directly with _____ or provide me with some ideas about how I can support the work that you are doing with _____?"

Well-intentioned administrators may inadvertently place mentors in positions that strain confidentiality. Mentors may want to be prepared with statements such as these that help honor their colleagues' confidence and that show respect for the administrator who wants to gather feedback on a teacher's performance. Moreover, there are appropriate places for administrators and mentors to have conversations about instructional practice, and there is no reason why a mentor and principal cannot address instructional challenges. But the hallway— where conversations are more than public—is out of bounds for such conversations.

Boundaries create identity, and a strong competency identity makes it unnecessary for the mentor to be reactive in complex situations. In the previous example, the assistant principal did not understand the appropriate boundary for conversations about a teacher, and Karen as the mentor, deflected the question in a professional manner. There are also legal limits to conversations, and parties involved in supporting teachers must understand appropriate subjects and options during public and private conversations about a teacher's classroom performance.

Principals need to protect mentors from these difficult conversations that might lead to a violation of trust, and many times mentors must guide principals. We recommend a set of clearly articulated communication guidelines to promote consistent and clear communication. For example, we endorse the following for mentors when speaking with building administrators about mentoring:

- Collect and speak "from" student performance data.

- Talk about the ways in which time was spent with teachers.

- Avoid evaluative language about teachers and the data collected.

- Discuss current mentoring strategies to improve instruction—on which the teacher is working (e.g., better planning, management strategies, more effective communication with parents, collaborative activities).

These guidelines provide factual points of departure for conversations that will keep the focus on instruction and progress. They also establish boundaries that assist with maintaining confidentiality while facilitating productive dialogue with the building administrator. Consider the following conversation with Doug, a high school principal, and Amanda, an instructional mentor, during their weekly thirty-minute conversation.

> This week the conversation focused on two special educators with whom Amanda had been working. The principal, Doug, began the conversation with an open-ended question, allowing Amanda to respond.
>
> "Well, how are they doing? Aren't they working on common assessments?"
>
> "They are working on a common assessment for writing, and during last week's inservice day, they worked hard on completing the free-response portion of their assessment. I provided some examples of assessments that they used."
>
> "And you are satisfied with how it is going? I mean our scores are not so good, and they need help in that area."
>
> "Last week we looked at last year's writing results and then took the strands that students did not perform well on, and then built the assessment to help us in that area."
>
> "When will they give the assessment? What's the plan again?"
>
> "Next week, and we plan to score together the tests at our next inservice."

This conversation enabled the mentor and principal to focus on instructional improvement. Note that throughout the conversation, the principal poses questions about the production of the test and the work that was to occur. Clearly, he names the challenge—to improve writing instruction. As mentor and instructional coach, Amanda created a safe environment for the special education teachers to develop a common writing assessment, and in her conversation with Doug, she stated facts and delineated a timeline for administering, scoring, and then possibly analyzing the test. Note, too, that Amanda's responses were direct and precise. There was no need for posturing or avoiding the questions posed by the principal. Using the guidelines stated earlier, they talked with transparency about teachers in the building— teachers who fully understood that they were being talked about. In this case, boundaries helped create solidarity.

⋙ · Support and Evaluation for Mentors · ⋙

The quality of mentoring depends on the fluid exchange of new information about teaching and learning. As with any profession, mentors will need to grow, develop skills, and practice their craft. Principals need to be mindful of this need and provide mentors with professional growth opportunities. Whether that means purchasing professional books for mentors to read or supporting mentors who want to attend professional conferences, mentors need opportunities to improve the quality of their work with beginning teachers.

To a large extent, the relationship created between the mentor and the person being mentored is dependent on the quality of school administrator support. The amount of collaboration or work time after or before school depends on the administrator's level of support for the mentoring process. And it is often the administrator who determines areas of focus and expected results for the mentor's work.

Frequently, and especially in smaller school districts, the building principal assumes responsibility for evaluating the mentor. And for many principals, the evaluating of a mentor is not as straightforward a process as the evaluating of a typical classroom teacher. What constitutes success as a mentor? Do we count the number of interactions or class visits for the mentor? How does student academic performance calculate into determining whether or not a mentor is successful?

These questions and others should guide those responsible for developing an evaluation tool for mentors. Many mentors with whom we have worked report little or no evaluation of their work. This is tragic, because without evaluation, mentors often have no mechanism for gauging their performance. Mentors certainly do need to be evaluated if they are to improve their craft. As a result, an evaluation instrument with clear criteria and guidelines needs to be developed.

Consider the assessment model that one urban school district developed for its mentoring and coaching program (see Figure 11.1). The model, which is a work in progress for the district's coordinators, contains four domains for assessment, including Planning and Preparation, Coaching/Mentoring Interactions, Facilitation of Adult Learning, and Professional Responsibilities. These domains provide both mentor and administrator helpful guidance when determining roles and responsibilities. It also helps clarify basic elements for assessing mentoring performances.

Figure 11.1 Assessment Model for Evaluating Mentors and Coaches

Domain 1: Planning and Preparation	Domain 2: Coaching/Mentoring Interactions
Incorporates Knowledge of Building, District, and Standards • Curriculum and teaching standards • Goals and initiatives • School and staff culture **Designs Professional Support** • Teacher-centered support • Data-driven support • Selection of coaching/mentoring goals **Organizes Time and Resources** • Time • Resources	**Builds Professional Relationships** • Demonstrates ability to work with a variety of teaching styles and proficiencies • Relationships based on credibility, trust, and confidentiality **Matches Coaching/Mentoring Support Functions to Circumstances** • Coaching • Collaborating • Consulting • Navigates among and between coaching/mentoring support functions **Utilizes Coach/Mentor Observation Cycle** • Planning conversation • Classroom observation • Reflective conversation **Uses Data to Drive Coaching/Mentoring Interactions** • Uses formal and informal sources of student, teacher, and/or building data

Domain 3: Facilitation of Adult Learning	Domain 4: Professional Responsibilities
Communicates Effectively • Clear and accurate oral and written communication • Timely **Uses Effective Strategies for Adult Learners** • Presentation of content and skilled facilitation • Learning environment **Provides Variety of Learning Opportunities** • Three venues (one on one, small group, large group) • Differentiated learning experiences **Demonstrates Flexibility and Responsiveness** • Feedback to and from stakeholders • Monitors and adjusts instruction/ activities • Persistence	**Reflects on Coaching/Mentoring Effectiveness** • Personal reflection • Collaborative reflection • Use in future coaching/mentoring **Maintains Appropriate Records** • Coaching/mentoring calendar/schedule • Coaching/mentoring log **Communicates in the Educational Environment** • Information about the instructional program, instructional strategies, and/or students • Communicating in a professional environment **Contributes to the School and District** • Relationships with colleagues • Shows professionalism • Student and best practice • Continuous professional growth

We suggest, too, that any evaluation tool, such as the one delineated in Figure 11.1, includes requirements for goal setting. Goal setting is at the heart of any learning enterprise, and when mentors write and work toward goals, they demonstrate for their colleagues their own commitment to improvement. Moreover, goals help to focus work.

Consider Tami's statement about a goal she set for the school year. As an instructional mentor in a large school district, she was provided an evaluation rubric that included criteria for both goal setting and for gathering data when working with beginning teachers. In her second year as a mentor, Tami reflected:

> My goals reflect the things I want to improve . . . I spent my summer reading about methods for collecting qualitative data. Last year I sat in classroom after classroom and took a few notes on what I was seeing, and then I would talk with the teacher about my notes. This year I want to gather data in a systematic fashion. You know, using charts, counting the number of student responses, focusing on one or two students' time on task. This year, I want the data to talk loud so that I can do more listening and guiding than directing. So that is one of my goals.

Practicing mentors report that that they receive little tangible information about whether they are actually helping teachers with whom they are working to improve. One way for mentors to assess whether they are supporting teachers is to develop goals like Tami did and to reflect on those goals as they work with new colleagues.

An effective assessment process will include frequent opportunities for mentors to voice their concerns and receive feedback on their performances. Mentoring, like teaching, is not algorithmic: Mentoring varies daily and differs from teacher to teacher. As a result, mentors will need frequent opportunities to take stock of their own work to recalibrate their mentoring. Frequent meetings with an administrator responsible for evaluating the mentor will help. Previously, we heard Doug and Amanda discuss the activities of a pair of special educators with whom Amanda was working. This weekly fifteen- to thirty-minute interaction provided the principal, Doug, and Amanda, the mentor, with time to discuss current activities and address questions and areas of concern.

Finally, quality feedback depends greatly on a clear and sensible set of performance criteria. As in the assessment model presented in Figure 11.1, these criteria should be clearly articulated and understood by all parties involved in the assessment process. Additionally, when considering a summative or concluding evaluation tool, we believe it important to differentiate between coherence and prescription. Subscription to performance standards differs from prescription, and we believe that when evaluating mentors, it is important for evaluators to look for contributions in terms of the mentor's professional growth and the continuous changes occurring in the beginning teacher with whom the mentor is working. In other words, whereas guidance in terms of clear criteria is important, an overly prescriptive evaluation tool might restrict a mentor's performance and limit the possibilities for the mentor to effect lasting change in new colleagues.

✎ · Summary · ✎

We began this chapter suggesting that the relationship between mentor and administrator is frequently complex. Mentors and school administrators must determine roles and boundaries for successful collaboration. Capacity to improve instruction, after all, is dependent, to a large extent, on the quality of the relationships in a school. And strong relationships, especially when considering mentors and administrators, are built on solid communication strategies. Avoiding the "communication triangle," where the mentor functions as a conduit between teacher and administrator, is critical. Moreover, when mentors and administrators develop a set of guidelines for talking about their work with colleagues, confidentiality and trust can be maintained. Finally, the work of a mentor must be assessed, and the assessment model provided in this chapter goes far in terms of setting a course for understanding quality mentoring performances. It is through thoughtful and systematic evaluation that professionals reflect on and improve their performance, and it is through a clear understanding of the mentor's roles and responsibilities that capacity for lasting change in schools will increase.

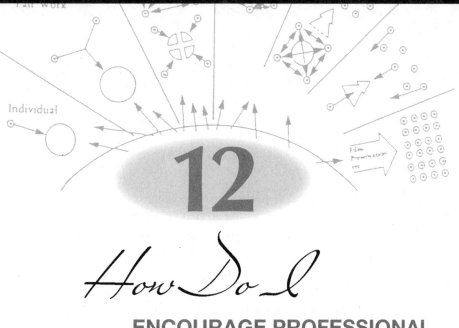

12

How Do I

ENCOURAGE PROFESSIONAL DEVELOPMENT?

Each time a person completes a novel, a research project or a composition,
he/she discovers new, unresolved issues that have to be addressed.
In creative work, a single product is just a temporary resting place
in the continuing and demanding process.

—Vera John-Steiner, *Notebooks of the Mind*

Chapters 3 and 4 suggested that in preparing for mentoring, you should consider how to encourage beginning teachers to develop their skills and abilities. Without a doubt, a mentor can significantly influence the beginning teacher's degree of involvement in professional activities and the quality of knowledge and satisfaction he or she gains in the application of that professional knowledge in the classroom. The mentor's role is indeed crucial to the beginning teacher's professional development.

For the beginning teacher, professional development involves learning about new teaching strategies and techniques and implementing and integrating these strategies and techniques into classroom practice. Mentors can encourage new teachers to stretch their understanding and support them as they practice what they have learned.

Collaboration is a fruitful way to promote and sustain professional development. When mentors assist, support, and guide professional inquiry and development, they steer newcomers toward enduring scholarly success. They can model productive behavior and, because they adhere to professional expectations, demonstrate an honorable intellectual ethic.

✑ · Individual Professional Development Plan · ✑

District-based mentoring programs for beginning teachers often include generic "one-shot" workshops that focus on particular teaching strategies or practices. The assumption guiding many of these workshops is that all beginning teachers require the same kind of support and information in order to succeed in their classrooms, that every teacher, for example, needs classroom management strategies or practice with new curriculum materials. But most of these inservices overlook the individual needs of beginning teachers. Some new teachers require assistance in managing the classroom more productively, others in organizing and planning instruction. Because they work closely with beginning teachers, mentors can better determine individual needs and develop specific plans to meet those needs.

This is not to suggest that generic district- or school-sponsored workshops and programs cannot be useful; many are very productive. But not every beginning teacher will benefit from these activities, and it is important to blend district or school objectives with the beginning teacher's needs and professional development goals.

We recommend that with the help of a mentor, each beginning teacher draw up a comprehensive individual professional development plan (IPDP), one that takes the various needs of that particular teacher into account. Such a process-oriented plan supports both short- and long-term goals that focus directly on teaching skills, strategies, and knowledge.

An Individual Professional Development Plan includes three basic components: (1) goals, (2) pathways, and (3) the portfolio. Beginning teachers need goals to determine what they want to learn and professional development pathways to meet their stated goals. The portfolio, which may contain lesson plans, units, activities, notes, letters, and pictures, documents intellectual and professional progress toward meeting goals and can be used as a tool for reflection and further goal setting.

Each beginning teacher's plan will be distinctive yet may include some of the same goals and approaches. An IPDP should not conflict with a district or school mentoring program with specific objectives, programs, or goals; it should, in fact, complement such a program by enabling individual beginning teachers to focus on district objectives as well as on their own individual classroom challenges and scholarly goals.

Professional Development Goals

Not enough has been written about beginning teachers and setting goals to guide future professional development. After they have signed a teaching contract, beginning teachers are often informed by district personnel about particular professional development requirements and about when and where this development will occur. Usually the "when" and the "where" mean district-sponsored professional development activities or inservice programs that focus on very general aspects of teaching. Not every activity in a general inservice workshop or program, however, will meet the professional development needs of each beginning teacher. This is why we suggest that you assist the beginning teacher to meet the school or district expectations and to augment these activities with individual professional development plans.

Short-Term Goals

Short-term goals are those that can be achieved in a relatively brief amount of time—an hour, a day, a week, or a month. They focus on immediately useful tasks or teaching strategies. Early in a beginning teacher's career, especially during the "survival stages," mentors may wish to direct her attention to achieving short-term goals. Short-term goals reinforce the significance of setting goals, build confidence to undertake more challenging goals, and often lead directly to long-term goals, some of which will guide professional development activities for years to come.

For Sandra, a beginning third-grade teacher, short-term goals provided comfort and direction. Her mentor, Marge, a twenty-five-year veteran, helped Sandra set her short-term goals. Because of the demand for new teachers, Sandra had been hired directly after earning her B.A. from a reputable university. She had not completed a certification program and was using a temporary certificate. Sandra knew she wanted to teach and was delighted to have an opportunity to work with a third-grade class, yet she understood very little about how to teach or assess reading. In her journal, she wrote, "I want to be the very best teacher for my students. They are counting on me to be the very best. One area that I need help in is teaching reading, especially with running records and other strategies." For Sandra, Marge's expertise became an invaluable resource.

During the second month of classes, Marge visited with Sandra in her classroom. Sandra was in a panic about reading instruction. In tears, she told Marge that she felt she was cheating her students, whose abilities ranged from at-risk to gifted.

During lunch, Marge reassured Sandra that she wasn't cheating her students and that as a teacher she did have much to offer. As they talked about the problem, they developed a couple of short-term goals: First, Sandra would learn how Marge completed running records with her students; second, Sandra would actually conduct a running record in Marge's classroom, with her supervision. With these goals in place, they had a plan, and with a plan, there would be productive effort and action. Marge encouraged Sandra to record these short-term goals and file them in a goals section in her professional portfolio (see Figure 12.1).

Figure 12.1 Individual Professional Development Plan

(To be revised quarterly and included in your portfolio)

Teacher _____ Date _____

School _____ Class or Grade _____

Short-Term Goals

1.
2.
3.
4.

Plan of Action (Briefly describe your plan or pathway to meet one or more of these goals.)

Long-Term Goals

1.
2.
3.
4.

Plan of Action (Briefly describe your plan or pathway to meet one or more of these goals.)

Long-Term Goals

A mentor offers a new colleague a seasoned perspective on the benefits of setting short-term goals and working to achieve them. Mentors also demonstrate the necessity for long-term goals, which reach beyond the immediate concerns of the classroom and may lead to improved classroom performance. Unlike short-term goals, however, they are developed with an eye to the future—a year, five years, or even longer.

A few months later, Marge encouraged Sandra to set a long-term goal that would expand her knowledge of teaching reading to both first- and second-language learners and dialect learners. With her mentor's support and guidance, Sandra set two long-term goals: (1) to earn a master's degree in teaching literacy, with a specialization in reading, and (2) to learn more about using children's literature to teach reading to second-language learners.

During their conversations, Marge suggested that Sandra enroll in a master's program offering courses on the theory and practice of reading. She also urged Sandra to take advantage of a weeklong summer reading symposium, cosponsored by the school district and a local university, which focused on using complete works of children's literature to teach reading skills and strategies. While attending the symposium, Sandra could also earn credit that would count toward an advanced degree in reading.

Long-term goals form an integral part of the teacher's professional development plan, one that they will update over the span of their career. Sandra's individual goals, for example, are linked directly to the perceived needs of her classroom. At the beginning of every semester, Sandra may return to her list of goals, update them, and determine what specific course of action to undertake next.

Here are a few ways that you, as an individual or team mentor, can promote goal setting:

- Encourage consideration of both long- and short-term goals.
- Monitor these goals frequently and encourage revision.
- Celebrate the achievement of short- and long-term goals.
- Assist the beginning teacher to record these goals in a professional portfolio.
- Share your own professional development goals with the beginning teacher and talk about how they have changed over time.

Mentors set the course for professional development by emphasizing the importance of setting goals and extending the learning these goals represent. With Marge's help, Sandra mapped out a productive course of action.

✐ · Professional Development Pathways · ✐

A pathway is a tool—such as inservice programs, conferences, workshops, professional organizations, college coursework, and books—that promotes and enhances professional development. But pathways alone aren't enough to make the professional development experience rewarding. What beginning teachers need more than anything else is support and guidance as they develop their own professional skills and knowledge. This is where mentors can be most helpful. With their support, guidance, and feedback, new teachers will discover individual pathways to professional development.

District- or School-Sponsored Mentoring Programs

Individual schools or districts usually offer their beginning teachers many opportunities to develop professionally. In discussing district- or school-sponsored development activities with the beginning teacher, characterize these workshops or seminars as professional, intellectual, and social opportunities. Such programs offer an opportunity to learn about the school and its culture, consider complicated educational concepts, or learn about the school's strategic agenda or the instructional plan for change. Finally, inservices provide opportunities to link information to a broader professional development agenda.

> Jessy, a beginning fifth-grade teacher, had to be convinced. During student teaching she had heard stories about district inservice programs. "I mean, my cooperating teacher told me that those programs were a waste of time. I need that time to get my lessons ready. I'm one day ahead of the students! I can't afford to waste my time."

At the start, you may want to attend district- or school-sponsored inservice programs or workshops with the beginning teacher as Jessy's mentor, Cindy, did, even though the information was of less use to her than to Jessy. Beginning teachers like Jessy need to see veteran teachers engaged in inservice programs. It is also comforting to sit next to a trusted friend at one of these events, especially if the workshop is interactive. You also may want to allocate time in your schedule, either at lunch or after school, to discuss the program and the material presented.

Professional Organizations

Membership in a professional organization can be a source of substantive professional development. By joining an organization such as the National Council of Teachers of

English, the National Academy of Science, or the International Reading Association, new teachers have a way to participate in the conversations of the profession. Membership also carries privileges. Most national organizations offer members subscriptions to content-related publications and newsletters, which provide valuable information on developments or debates in the profession and professional conferences.

Encourage your new colleagues to join at least one professional organization and to explore what it has to offer. (If you haven't joined one, this is an excellent time to do so.)

Professional Conferences

Although many school districts sponsor internal professional development programs, attending a local or a professional conference can be an immensely productive and rewarding experience. These conferences provide information, present opportunities for participating in conversations about innovative classroom procedures, structures, and curricula, and can lead to new acquaintances with other professionals.

There are many ways to make these conferences useful professional development activities for the beginning teacher. Professional organizations promote local, regional, and national conferences in their publications; information is relatively easy to locate. A beginning teacher's short- or long-term goals may lead directly to a conference on a specific subject. Try to attend at least the first conference with the beginning teacher. A well-run event will offer more sessions than anyone can take in, so your guidance on session selection may be of great help. You and your new colleague could plan to split up and attend different conference presentations, then meet later to pool information and ideas.

Encourage the beginning teacher to get involved in organizing or planning a local or state conference. Leaders of these organizations are always looking for members who will contribute time, energy, and skills. Those who are involved often pay a reduced attendance fee.

> Cassandra, a new second-grade teacher, found attending the spring California Association of Teachers of English conference a wonderful resource. "That was a great experience for me," she told her mentor Jackie during their joint planning time. "I never realized that there are so many teachers who have the same interests and questions about teaching that I do. I exchanged email addresses with three or four teachers I met, and one of them is going to email me information about a wonderful listserv she belongs to. I'm ready for next year's conference already!"

Present a paper, curricular innovation, or research project with your beginning colleague. As a form of collaboration, copresenting with a beginning teacher can provide valuable interaction and promote learning of the highest order. You emphasize and model the importance of thinking, working, and sharing concerns and ideas about the classroom with other teachers.

Karen, a beginning teacher, and Daniel, her mentor, documented and planned a presentation on classroom practice. Karen was eager to try out innovative approaches in teaching literature in her classroom. At the university, Karen had read about reader-response theory and the ways in which literature circles (Daniels 2001) could introduce such a theoretical approach into the classroom. In one of her university literature courses, she had also had the opportunity to read, respond, and react to literature within a literature circle.

In reviewing the middle school curriculum, however, Karen grew concerned: "There's no mention of literature circles in the curriculum guide." In fact, many teachers at the school hadn't even heard of this approach. Still interested in implementing the innovation, she set a goal in her IPDP to implement literature circles even though she did not know if this method was an acceptable practice at her school.

Daniel, Karen's mentor, began the school year with a plan to use literature circles in his sixth-grade language arts classes. Daniel had been intrigued for some time by the whole notion of literature circles and wondered how he could introduce them in his seventh-grade language arts classes. He had read articles in professional journals about the promise of such an approach and had wanted to try out the strategy in his teaching.

During one of their conversations, Daniel suggested that they collaborate on literature circles. They would share ideas, exchange materials, and document their work for future reference. For a semester, they both kept track of their experiences with literature circles in a dialogue journal. Daniel wrote about his teaching one week; then it was Karen's turn to record her observations and thoughts.

After a semester's worth of working with literature circles and writing about them, Karen and Daniel proposed a session to a state-level conference, highlighting the ways that they implemented literature circles and the methods they had used to assess students' scholarly progress as a result of the literature circles. Using student work, self-generated performance assessment, and their dialogue journal, they shared their perspectives about the new innovation at the conference. After the presentation, session participants thanked Karen and Daniel for their work and willingness to share their methods and discoveries.

University or College Courses

Many of our new colleagues, recent graduates of university teacher education programs, dread the thought of opening yet another textbook or attending yet another class. Most have invested four or more years in their undergraduate education and thousands of dollars for required courses, books, and supplies. By this time, most are ready for a role change. They are neither emotionally nor financially ready for an immediate return to graduate coursework. Teaching during the day and taking courses at night or on weekends may make for a very exhausting schedule. Facing the demands of the classroom and graduate study, these new teachers tire quickly and easily. Often, pressed for time, they rush through their lesson planning or hurry through the assignments for their university coursework. Neither is creatively productive.

Considering the high rates at which beginning teachers leave the profession, we suggest that mentors not recommend graduate work until after the beginner has acquired a full sense of the curriculum goals and a clear understanding of the rigors of teaching. Returning to graduate classes after earning a teaching credential, however, is vital to the beginning teacher's professional development. We recommend that these new colleagues set long-term goals for graduate study and enroll in a degree program a year or two after they begin teaching.

After a year of teaching seventh-grade language arts, Ted decided he wanted to pursue a graduate degree. "I love to learn, and I am aware that many new teachers drop out after a short time in the classroom. I need to stay fresh, up-to-date, and graduate school, I think, can help me stay intellectually alive." For Ted, graduate school offered a chance for intellectual refreshment and easy access to research and information that would, in his estimation, sustain him.

Many universities offer veteran and beginning teachers opportunities to study in professional development schools or in subject-matter projects, both usually affiliated with a university offering graduate degree programs. Learning in such programs involves collaboration and collegiality that can enhance the professional life of an educator.

State Subject-Matter Projects

National and state subject-matter projects (such as the National Writing Project) provide some of the finest professional development opportunities available. We support these projects as exciting professional development pathways because of our own experiences with them and have suggested them to those we have mentored and taught.

Subject-matter projects offer terrific professional development opportunities for practicing teachers. Most projects are structured along the "teachers teaching teachers" model, giving beginning teachers sustained opportunities to talk with and learn from the most capable of their peers. And since subject-matter projects are usually conducted during three to five weeks of the summer, they are especially suited to teachers.

It was Nina's first year of teaching in an urban school that had earned a rough reputation. She had recently finished her coursework in education and was ready for the new challenge of teaching five ninth-grade language arts classes—or at least she thought she was. Before assuming her teaching position, she had been a successful undergraduate, earning As in nearly all her classes. Student teaching had been a positive, rewarding experience as well. Yet Nina spent the first semester struggling to stay just one day, and in some cases one hour, ahead of her students. She reflected on her situation in her journal: "I'm spending long hours after school and on the weekends getting activities and lessons ready. But I am not satisfied with the quality of writing that many of my students are coming up with. Do you think that I should try a writer's workshop? Will a workshop help them to boost their writing?"

Irene, Nina's mentor, had much to offer. After reading Nina's journal entry, Irene talked with Nina at great length about transforming her classroom into a reading and writing workshop. Irene understood that Nina's attempt to create a workshop atmosphere in her classes at the midyear point would demand more time and energy than she had; she was already logging long hours in preparing for her daily lessons.

Irene wisely encouraged Nina to experiment with ideas for workshop activities during the remainder of the year. She also suggested that Nina make designing and teaching a workshop format part of her IPDP. Nina did, and she also established several goals: to attend the National Writing Project summer workshops and to continue to learn about workshops through her professional reading. Irene recommended Nancie Atwell's (1998) classic *In the Middle* and Lois Bridges Bird's (1997) *Writing as a Way of Knowing*, both of which offer practical ideas and suggestions for teaching reading and writing in a workshop format.

Professional Texts and Journals

Beginning teachers like Nina can also learn from professional texts and journals, which focus on the immediate concerns of the classroom. Here, beginning and mentor teachers encounter the latest innovations, trends, debates, and research in their fields.

"I couldn't believe what I was reading," Danielle, a beginning teacher, wrote in a journal entry about the first few chapters of Sondra Perl and Nancy Wilson's (1986) *Through Teachers' Eyes*. "These are veteran teachers who are learning as they go. Take Ross, for instance. He was a veteran teacher who just had a bad year. It pains me to know that he had such a tough time with the changes he made, but it's comforting to know that older teachers struggle, too. Is that bad of me to say that?"

Schools rarely build in enough time for sustained reading of professional materials. Instructional time zips by, and it is rare to find even a quiet moment, let alone a short block of time, to reflect on teaching practices. Because of the often frenetic pace of most school days, beginning teachers like Danielle need to make time for professional reading, and it helps if you can demonstrate ways to do so. You might also try reading the same journal articles or texts for joint discussion. Some schools do have ongoing study groups in which staff members meet on a regular basis, usually before or after school and sustained by food and drink, to discuss a professional article or book. If your school does not have such a group in place and you think it might be a productive enterprise enthusiastically received, why not propose setting one up? Start small by planning a limited number of sessions, and see how it goes.

Classroom-Based Inquiry

Conducting a classroom-based research project with a beginning teacher may be one of the most rewarding aspects of mentoring. Through these projects, beginning and veteran teachers apply a careful, critical method to look at their teaching and their students' learning. The very acts of documenting and reflecting on classroom action can result in deeper understanding.

Class-based research can be guided by personal questions about teaching or learning. How do students use the Internet as they conduct research? How do students use my written responses to revise their essays? What is the relationship between my district's content standards and the stated curriculum? Or research can be linked to the educational reform agenda of a school or district. A school district, for example, might be experimenting with a particular curriculum or instructional innovation. Research findings can be used to determine the effectiveness of the change or reform or to assist individual teachers in improving their instruction and setting goals for professional development.

Equally important for the beginning teacher is the chance to work directly with the skilled educator doing the research. (We would not recommend that a beginning teacher conduct classroom-based inquiry without assistance.) What energizes and sustains classroom professionals is collaboration with seasoned colleagues who share similar concerns and interests. Reflective discussions and conversations between class-based researchers may also assist in the interpretation of complex research data. In fact, these conversations may be more important than the actual writing of the research.

To get you started, we recommend two accessible texts that provide information about how to conduct classroom-based inquiry with the beginning teacher: Richard Sagor (2000), *Guiding School Improvement with Action Research*; Ruth Shagoury Hubbard and Brenda Miller Power (2003), *The Art of Classroom Inquiry*.

❧ · The Professional Development Portfolio · ❧

The final, yet perhaps most essential, component of the beginning teacher's IPDP is the portfolio. Anything the beginning teacher generates in the classroom or during teaching or professional development activities can be included: a piece of writing from a student; an assignment sheet; pictures of classroom activities; videotapes of teaching; photographs of students, volunteers, or tutors; personal writing; lesson plans; and units that have been taught. Collected and organized in the portfolio, artifacts like these can point toward important discoveries about future goals and pathways.

As a mentor, encourage the beginning teacher to use the portfolio to document personal academic achievements and accomplishments as well as professional progress. Portfolios link our histories as students to our current work as teachers, which is rooted in our autobiographies, our personal circumstances, our deep commitments, our emotional investments, and our social context. Urge the beginning teacher to include artifacts that represent all aspects of life. That's what Allison, a beginning seventh-grade science teacher, did with the assistance of her mentor, Tony.

> Tony assisted Allison in setting up a portfolio. He recommended that she purchase a three-ring binder and start collecting records and artifacts during the first couple of months of her teaching. He also recommended that she allocate space for both short- and long-term goals and for professional development materials provided by the school district. Beyond these suggestions, however, Tony simply encouraged Allison to select the personal and professional artifacts she thought best represented her as a developing science teacher and her students as budding scientists.
>
> Toward the end of the first semester, Tony and Allison met to talk about her portfolio and to plan and revise her professional development plan. Allison displayed her folder, in which she had included an assortment of items—pictures, descriptions of experiments, assessments she had given her students, and the record of two research projects she conducted as an undergraduate.

Eventually, they focused on the lab reports Allison asked her students to write during the term. "I want to learn about ways to use and teach writing in the science classroom," Allison told Tony, who recommended that she document her goals in her portfolio; he also recommended that she read several articles and books that would guide her in using writing more effectively in the science classroom.

Tony did more than simply assist Allison in her reflection and goal setting. He also shared his own portfolio and professional development goals. "Well, I've jotted down a few goals, too. Here are mine. What do you think about my second long-term goal, integrating district-mandated science standards? My plan is to review my curriculum and then map the standards that line up with the materials—that's on my list of things to do this summer."

By sharing his own portfolio and his own goals, Tony showed respect for his junior colleague—who might, as he implied, have something to teach him. Such reciprocity is very important. Moreover, clearly keeping and reviewing a professional portfolio is beneficial throughout a teaching career. Even Tony, an award-winning teacher of fifteen years, still had goals and plans for further developing his professional knowledge and abilities.

To make productive use of their portfolios, beginning teachers like Allison need time to review and reflect on their contents. Simply leafing through various items can make connections and inspire new investigations, as Tony and Allison's conversation attests. In the case of team mentors, the team can provide joint portfolio input, presenting different options for the beginning teacher to consider.

Without reflection and analysis, however, portfolios are simply containers destined to collect dust on a classroom shelf. There is also a danger in too narrowly conceptualizing portfolios in classrooms and mentor programs. Some states may require beginning teachers to compile a portfolio with artifacts and commentaries proving their having met state standards. Mentors can greatly assist in this process. However, using a portfolio to "prove" or "showcase" is only half the story. Portfolios are made powerful in the hands of their users when they become tools for generating thinking.

✂ · Summary · ✂

By assisting beginning teachers to develop an Individual Professional Development Plan that includes goals, pathways, and a portfolio, a mentor helps to connect ideas across issues, topics, and practices. Work on Individual Professional Development Plans may also lead to substantive collaboration with benefits for beginner and mentor alike.

The finest, most rewarding professional development generally occurs by working and learning alongside trusted colleagues. Teaching all day in a classroom overflowing with students can be a very lonely professional experience. New and veteran teachers alike often feel isolated and at times unsupported, especially when implementing new curricula, standards, or assessments. A mentor's support and guidance is essential to the beginning teacher's continued professional development. With years of experience and knowledge as a guide, a mentor can provide information and direction that will lead the beginning teacher to new investigations and strategies, new professional sources and organizations, and new commitment and resolve to improve curriculum and instruction.

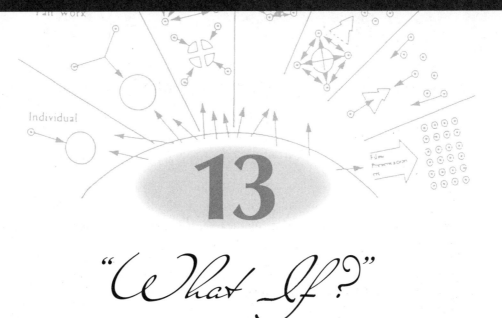

13

"What If?"

QUESTIONS FROM MENTORS

Dolores, a student teaching supervisor from a nearby university, stuck her head in Ian Chandler's classroom and announced, "Ian, just the person I was looking for! I'm hoping to talk you into becoming a mentor teacher for one of our university students."

"Really?" said Ian. "Do you think I'm ready for that type of responsibility? I've only been in the district three years, and there are some days when I feel I can hardly handle my own teaching, much less help someone else with theirs."

"I wouldn't be here if I didn't think you were up to the challenge. And if you've got a minute, I'd be happy to sit down with you and field some of the questions or concerns you might have."

University supervisors are always on the lookout for new mentors for their student teachers, just as administrators in school districts around the country are always considering who among their teaching staff could successfully manage the mentorship of a new teacher. However, while many teachers are pleased to be asked, they often have questions about what mentoring might involve. This chapter is an overview of some of the questions posed by mentor teachers who are working with beginning teachers. First, we focus on questions that apply to any mentoring situation, then we discuss the student teacher experience, and finally, we consider questions related to mentoring the beginning teacher.

✂ • Questions for Any Mentoring Situation • ✂

Question 1: *What are the most important attributes of an effective mentor teacher?*

Content knowledge is always important, but more important are flexibility, open-mindedness, and a willingness to engage in active communication with the beginning teacher.

A flexible, open-minded mentor encourages colleagues to experiment, even if they make mistakes or, sometimes, fail as they introduce new classroom activities. Mentors model flexibility in how they respond to the small crises that occur during a typical school day—fire drills, pep assemblies, inconvenient intercom announcements, and so on. They also affirm the courage of beginning teachers in taking risks and stretching themselves professionally.

Collegiality is an important aspect of school life just as it is in any community. Regular communication is a necessity if teachers are to be true colleagues. Most beginning teachers are eager to engage in this kind of interaction with a mentor. Some mentors try to find time for thoughtful conversation every day. Even if a novice teacher is reluctant to analyze her classroom performance, an effective, trusted mentor will be able to initiate this kind of discussion.

These conversations are also beneficial to the mentor, who will learn to recognize when the new teacher is feeling comfortable and when she is having qualms. Sometimes beginning teachers look competent even as they may be experiencing underlying uneasiness; an experienced teacher's encouragement and openness to discussing these concerns may be very liberating for both. A sense of humor doesn't hurt, either!

Question 2: *What if I don't know enough? What if I'm not really ready for this role?*

This is a common concern, especially among younger members of the profession when accepting their first mentoring assignment. Occasionally, principals/

administrators will encourage a teacher to become a mentor before that teacher feels ready for the responsibility. This is the exception, however, and actually indicates satisfaction with what the prospective mentor has already accomplished in the school.

Of all the fears about becoming a mentor, this one probably has the least foundation. You do know more than the new teacher for whom you will have responsibility, because you are already in the classroom and have survived the first years of your career. In addition, it is not necessary to know everything or experience everything about teaching before becoming a mentor.

Teachers who continue to feel concerned about their readiness may want to think about the following philosophical questions:

First, have you developed a strong philosophy of education? Are you clear about the current decisions you are making in your classroom, for you as teacher and for your students? How does your philosophy of teaching affect the instructional choices and management decisions you have made in various courses? If you have decided on a student-centered classroom, for example, what beliefs about education led you to that choice? Or, if you've chosen an assertive disciplinary approach with your second graders, why did you make that decision? Our beliefs must underlie the decisions we make in our classrooms, and we must be able to articulate these beliefs to the new teachers we mentor.

Second, how comfortable will you be sharing your everyday practice, both the high points and the low? An important component of serving as mentor is being able to talk openly about your teaching experiences with your beginning teacher. Will you be willing to discuss the mistakes you have made—and do make—in classroom management? Will you feel awkward sharing your concerns about some of the approaches you've used to teach various concepts? You will need to resolve these issues before you accept a position as a mentor.

When you have considered your own teaching philosophy, here are some further questions to consider:

- Are you generally comfortable with classroom management? Are students nearly always on task and actively engaged in a learning environment?

- Do most students respond positively to your instruction?

- Do you have an efficient routine in place for record keeping and other organizational matters?

- Do colleagues, administrators, and parents accept you as a professional?

- Do you have enough confidence in your own skills to be interested in new ideas about content and instruction?

If you feel reasonably competent in these areas, you are probably ready to take on the role of mentor. Remember, perfection is not a requirement!

Question 3: *What if I have reason to criticize my beginning teacher? Won't this be very awkward for both of us?*

Julie, a new teacher in the district, has begun wearing overalls to school. Some students have told her they think it's great that she's wearing clothes "like ours," but her mentor has also overheard other student comments ("What does she think she's doing? She's supposed to be a teacher, not a kid!"). When her mentor raises the issue, Julie responds, "It shouldn't matter what I wear as long as I'm getting my point across. Anyway, some of the other teachers in this school don't dress up."

All of us are conditioned not to mention personal issues to fellow professionals; however, newcomers to the profession may not understand the effect of their appearance, habits, or language on students' perceptions of them. Naturally, you will mention your concerns to your colleague as politely and quietly as possible, but it is your responsibility to mention them, especially if you see behavior that will reflect negatively on their interactions with students, parents, and administrators. Fortunately, these situations do not arise very often.

Mentoring the Student Teacher

You remember that first day as a student teacher. Would you really get along with your cooperating teacher? What if she never let you teach? And now, as you stand on the other side of the desk, you may be wondering whether someone else can come into your classroom and work effectively with your students. Here are some of the questions potential mentors of student teachers most often ask.

Question 1: *What if my students prefer the student teacher to me?*

This is a common concern of new mentors. It recognizes students' attraction to novelty in any form. Students may be especially interested in student teachers because they are young, have fresh ideas, or seem attuned to the music, television shows, books, and personal issues that are important to them. Sometimes student teachers have higher energy levels than their mentors, and that also sets them apart. Or students may be attracted to their typically more youthful fashion choices or manner of speaking.

A well-liked student teacher, however, actually enhances the class environment and helps to elicit even higher student achievement, but this fact does little to address the emotional reaction of the mentor teacher, who suddenly feels threatened, displaced, or out of style. Mentors should realize that in most cases, the situation rebalances quickly. Students will soon be able to sense the strengths of each of their teachers and appreciate both. In addition, once the student teacher assumes responsibility for the daily management of the classroom, students will realize that she expects the same type of accountability as the mentor teacher.

You should realize that this situation is typically short term and should not be seen as either a threat to you or a criticism of your teaching practices. However, if you suspect that it will remain uncomfortable, schedule your student teaching assignment for the fall semester so that both you and the student teacher will encounter students on the same footing.

Question 2: *What if the student teacher is poorly prepared?*

Or, can I really put this person in charge as my students prepare for high-stakes standardized tests? Juanita Sanchez, an experienced mentor teacher, has commented, "I'm concerned when the student teacher is either unprepared academically or has a poor attitude coming in, such as a student teacher saying, 'This is just time I have to put in [to finish my program].'" Further, many teachers are concerned that student teachers may not have the necessary background to help prepare secondary students for the kinds of high-stakes tests that have become so important in the wake of No Child Left Behind. Juanita speaks for many teachers in referring to her apprehensions about the preparation of student teachers. Most students are academically well prepared and personally well adjusted, but there are exceptions. Although most education programs have high standards and work extensively with their preservice teachers to promote accountability, in some cases, students who have met all the programmatic requirements must be allowed to student teach, whatever the reservations of the university supervisor. Normally, however, a university supervisor will alert the mentor to potential problems that may occur and keep in regular communication during the semester.

Realize, too, that some students who are well prepared may initially appear less competent because they are having problems with one or more of these areas:

Classroom Management. Consistent classroom management is probably the most common concern of both student and mentor teachers, and for good reason. Although most student teachers are academically well grounded in classroom management, nothing can adequately prepare them for the reality of an active classroom. How should the student teacher handle the girl who giggles incessantly? How does she respond to notes being passed surreptitiously from student to student? What should she do when she hears someone using profanity?

Classroom Routines. Student teachers may have problems at first in carrying out regular classroom routines, such as marking attendance and tardiness, handing out papers quickly and unobtrusively, or recording grades. It is difficult to resist intervening when you see your student teacher struggling to complete the daily attendance form while students become louder and more off task or returning newly graded papers or tests right before launching into a discussion of a complex subject. Or maybe you've noticed that the student teacher is allowing the class to engage in too much off-task conversation, something you monitor more closely.

Content Concerns. Your student teacher may not be as familiar with certain aspects of your subject matter as you expect. For example, what if the student teacher is leading the class in a discussion of why the atomic bomb was dropped on Hiroshima and Nagasaki, and one of the students asks the student teacher if the United States was aware that Japan was trying to surrender when the first bomb was dropped. The student teacher says, "Of course not," but you know that what she has said is not completely accurate. What do you do: jump into the discussion and offer the needed correction, slide a note to the student with the acceptable response, ask where the student got the information, bring the source to class for discussion, or sit there and squirm?

Testing Concerns. While many student teachers have taken the Iowa Tests of Educational Development, the SAT 9, or other state standard-driven competency tests and remember the types of questions that were asked, they may not be as clear as to how to prepare others for those tests. Further, mentor teachers often feel that they shouldn't take a student teacher during the semester the high-stakes test is offered because their students might be negatively impacted by a student teacher's lack of background in test prep. However, mentor teachers can provide important guidance in this arena by sharing materials and modeling test-taking techniques for their mentees as well as their secondary students. Also, new teachers to the field must understand how to balance curriculum issues with test-taking concerns, and mentors must be ready to respond to those issues and the inevitable questions that will arise.

Question 3: *What if the student teacher lacks basic grammatical skills?*

We would all like to believe that no student could reach the student teaching semester with poor basic skills in reading or writing. Unfortunately, some do. Consider the following scenarios:

Jeff, a student teacher in a ninth-grade classroom, prepares a handout for students that he intends to give them the following day. George, his mentor teacher, notices some glaring spelling and mechanical errors. George and Jeff review the handout and make the necessary corrections. Jeff apologizes for the errors, but two days later, he prepares another handout with similar errors.

During the first week of school, Lori, a student teacher, writes a letter to parents introducing herself and the work she intends to assign during her student teaching experience. Her mentor teacher, Carol, is very concerned about the number of grammatical errors she finds in the letter. Lori makes the suggested corrections cheerfully but does not seem particularly perturbed, noting to Carol that "everyone makes mistakes."

Janette, a student teacher, is working in a school that requires teachers to turn in weekly lesson plans and copies of tests, assignments, and so on. As the principal is perusing her plans, he notices a number of errors on the project sheet she is planning to discuss with students at the end of the week. He calls in both Janette and her mentor teacher and asks for an explanation. Both feel humiliated. Janette explains that she is dyslexic and has difficulty in this area; she promises she will pay more attention and have her mentor teacher proofread everything thoroughly before it is handed in to the principal. Throughout the rest of the semester, Janette's diligence pays off in the form of positive comments from her principal.

On occasion, a student teacher does not have the skills you would expect in a young professional. For example, the student teacher's inadequate spelling and grammar skills or poor reading ability may surprise you. While there are cases of dyslexia or other learning disabilities, it is unfortunately true that some students are not proficient. It is obviously unacceptable for any teacher to display such inadequacies publicly, especially in view of societal concerns about teacher education, so it is important that you set high standards and encourage the student teacher to meet them.

Every teacher has had the experience of making a spelling or grammatical error while writing on the board or preparing materials for students. Most of us have even had students catch the error before we did! However, in the case of Jeff and Lori above, we see student teachers with consistently poor basic skills who have not learned that they need to compensate for their weaknesses. In situations like these, it is the mentor teacher's obligation to insist that student teachers take the time to proofread their writing thoroughly or find an editor who can provide assistance. Student teachers who fail to see their poor skills as a serious issue must be reminded that parents, administrators, and students will question their professionalism if they produce flawed work.

Janette, in the third scenario, is struggling with a condition that predisposes her to make errors, but she realizes that she must take responsibility for them. Her attitude, obviously, is the appropriate one. Again, as a mentor, you will work with the university supervisor and insist that student teachers take their responsibility as role models in the area of basic skills very seriously. You might hesitate to be critical, but the situation requires clear and forthright standards.

Question 4: *What if the student teacher expresses personal moral, political, racial, or religious viewpoints in the classroom?*

Joe, a mentor teacher, considers his student teacher, Alex, to be a personable young man who really understands his subject matter. However, as the semester progresses, Joe notices that Alex rarely calls on students of diverse ethnic backgrounds during class discussion. When Joe asks Alex why, Alex seems sincerely surprised and promises to do better. A week later, when Joe points out that nothing has changed, Alex replies, "Well, they probably wouldn't know the answer anyway."

"Why wouldn't they have an answer?"

Alex laughs uncomfortably, "No reason, I guess."

We all dread the possibility of working with a colleague who is blatantly racist, sexist, or extreme in some manner. Alex's more subtle prejudice, however, may be more problematic because he may not at first admit—or even realize—that he is being unfair. Obviously, you must act decisively when a student teacher's attitudes are unacceptable. A candid discussion with the student teacher may help him realize the inappropriateness of his comments. Student teachers who harbor extreme opinions are unlikely to be allowed to student teach or to express such attitudes during the student teaching semester, but a student like Alex may not reveal his biases to the university instructors who approved his student teaching.

In a biology class, Maria, a student teacher, is lecturing on the origin of mankind. A student in the class raises her hand and says that her parents don't believe we evolved from an animal species. Maria glances at her mentor teacher for guidance.

This one is a tough call. Some teachers do not share their beliefs with students under any circumstances, even in response to direct questions, because they do not want to influence student decision making. Others have decided that on some issues, direct answers in response to questions are necessary. Still others feel that they should respond to all questions and that students may really want to know what teachers think about the subject. Then there is the teacher who brings up a controversial subject because he or she firmly believes in taking a stand on the issue. How do you help student teachers know how to respond?

During the course of the student teaching experience, the student teacher should go no further than the boundaries you set as the mentor. For example, if Maria's mentor has already established a pattern of openness with students, then Maria should feel comfortable giving her opinion while making it clear that it is her opinion. If the mentor deflects personal questions, Marie should do the same, even if she has decided that in her own classroom, she will adopt a different policy.

On some issues, such as religion, politics, or personal ethics, people have very different reactions. If, for example, Maria and her mentor strongly disagree about how to respond to students, the university supervisor should be invited to help resolve the problem.

Question 5: *What if the student teacher undermines me with my students?*

Student: *We're really glad that you're teaching now. Mrs. "Mentor" is so boring.*

Student teacher: *Well, you know, after you've been teaching the same thing year after year, it's hard to be too enthusiastic about it.*

You need to discuss mutual support, a professional issue, with the student teacher before the teaching experience begins. Just as children learn to play one parent against the other, students frequently try to play a student teacher against a mentor. Idealistic student teachers may be drawn into this game inadvertently because they want to be liked by the students. They must be made aware that everyone, including students, will be better off if the mentor and the student teacher present a unified front and actively support one another.

Student: *We're really glad that you're teaching now. Mrs. "Mentor" is so boring.*

Student teacher: *I think that Mrs. "Mentor" is really a wonderful teacher. Sometimes teachers have to discuss materials or concepts that may not be as interesting to begin with and aren't easy to teach in an exciting way. But I am glad you are enjoying my teaching so far.*

As a mentor teacher, you need to remember that you must give the same type of support to student teachers. The student teacher's worst nightmare is that you will undercut any authority or credibility he or she will ever have with students.

Advanced placement student: *You aren't really going to turn us over to the student teacher, are you? We want a "real" teacher. After all, we've exams to take, college courses to prepare for…*

Mentor: *Don't worry. If she's too terrible, I'll yank her.*

Although this scenario should be uncommon, we have heard versions of it from colleagues who act as mentors and from student teachers about whom such comments were made. Teachers and their students often develop remarkably strong bonds, which may make the student teacher feel like an outsider. At the same time, very goal-oriented students, who often choose courses and teachers to help them meet their goals and standards, may resent working with someone whom they feel is not as qualified, especially in advanced placement and college prep courses. As a mentor, you will need to work particularly hard to prepare students for the arrival of a new authority figure in the classroom even as you also provide support for all involved during the semester.

Advanced placement student: *You aren't really going to turn us over to the student teacher, are you? We want a "real" teacher. After all, we've exams to take, college courses to prepare for…*

Mentor: *Don't worry. I think you'll find Mr. McCoy very well qualified to work with us. In fact, since his coursework is more recent than mine, he will be able to provide you all with a sense of what college professors are looking for in your writing and in the type of class discussion they expect.*

Question 6: *How will things work out if I'm assigned a student teacher of the opposite gender?*

Susan, a student teacher, is offended by the way her mentor, Rick, talks to his students. He calls the girls "honey" but takes what she considers to be a more macho stance with the guys. Because Susan has researched gender issues for a college course, she feels strongly that students must be treated equally, regardless of gender.

Rick, on the other hand, thinks Susan is working so hard to treat everyone equally that she fails to see them as individuals. He thinks that gender equity includes recognizing differences between the sexes.

No one can deny the impact of gender in relationships. Many mentors prefer to work with student teachers of their own gender. They feel, for example, that they understand where other women are "coming from" in terms of concern for students, classroom management styles, content preferences, and so on. Many education programs support this viewpoint by making same-gender assignments or asking mentors about their preference in working with a student teacher. However, some mentors feel that working with a student of the opposite gender provides useful balance in the classroom. In these cases, certain common issues arise when teachers of opposite genders share a classroom.

In the example of Susan and Rick above, a first response should be open communication between the student teacher and her mentor. Each will probably need to modify expectations: Rick may want to suggest to Susan that she spend more time with individual students; he, in turn, might read one of the books about gender in the classroom that Susan finds especially informative. After their talk, both need to step back and consider positive aspects of the other's interactive style. They might also find it helpful to return to the subject throughout the semester and discuss how their perceptions are changing.

One of the advantages of a second set of eyes in the classroom is that you become aware of what you do well and what you need to work on to improve your teaching. Although you may have the best intentions when it comes to your students, there may be occasions when you unintentionally treat students in an inappropriate manner. David Sadker and Myra Sadker (1994) found that many teachers fail to see their own gender discrimination. For example, we may think that we're calling on girls and boys equally, but when we ask someone to track discussion patterns (see Chapter 5), we may find that we do not select students equitably. Student teachers may be willing to help you conduct the kind of teacher research you often have little time for during busy semesters.

Matt, a student teacher, is becoming increasingly impatient with what he sees as the weak management strategies of his mentor teacher, Julie. He feels she spends too much time listening to students' excuses and makes too many exceptions for hard-luck stories. Julie thinks Matt is being harsh and extremely strict with students, never taking into account how their personal lives may affect their performance in the classroom.

Male and female teachers often exhibit different classroom management styles. Student teachers may have different expectations about how to handle management, and this may lead to misunderstandings over interacting with students.

Although it may sound clichéd, the notion that women teachers are more nurturing and men teachers more task oriented has some validity. If teachers of different genders can remain open to a discussion of these variations, however, they may be able to enhance their own teaching styles with insights they have gained from their partner. In the case of Matt above, he and Julie need to realize the potential strengths and weaknesses of their individual management strategies. They might also consider how to balance their approaches: they may devise a structure within which students are expected to accomplish a certain amount of work but one that is also flexible enough for individualized instruction and interactions with the teacher.

Mia, a student teacher, is increasingly mystified about how Hal, her mentor teacher, controls the students in his class, especially because his manner seems exceptionally laid-back. As much as she tries to emulate his management style, she rarely gets the same results.

At six feet, four inches and 225 pounds, Hal is equally mystified, since students have always followed his instructions; he does admit, though, that Mia has followed all his management suggestions.

In this scenario, Hal's physical presence strongly influences the success of his classroom management strategies. Hal may therefore have difficulty recommending strategies that will work for a student teacher—male or female—whose stature is smaller than his. It might be most sensible for Hal to put Mia in touch with a colleague who has had to develop management strategies more conventionally.

Brian, a mentor teacher, is known around the school for his exciting science fiction course. His student teacher, Jessica, is uncomfortable with the type of material Brian has chosen because of its bloody, action-oriented content and has a difficult time reading it, much less leading a discussion about it.

Content issues—including books discussed and papers assigned—may also be affected by gender-related viewpoints. Although many school curricula designate texts for classroom instruction, teachers sometimes find opportunities to make their own choices. These choices often reflect their own personal preferences and may appeal more to one gender than to the other. Often, however, courses that attract almost exclusively male or female students may be serving a real need in a particular school.

In this situation, the problem arises because Jessica is uncomfortable with the materials Brian has chosen. As a mentor, Brian might let her choose a science fiction text she is more comfortable teaching. On the other hand, it is his course, and she may simply have to accept the fact that all teachers on occasion have to teach material they would not have chosen themselves.

Angela, a mentor teacher, emphasizes expressive writing assignments that al- low students to explore and communicate their feelings, something her student teacher, Brad, finds "touchy-feely" and devoid of meaningful learning.

Once again, balance and open communication are crucial. In this case, some students probably prefer the expressive writing Angela advocates, while others undoubtedly feel more comfortable with the fact-based, expository writing Brad assigns. Obviously, a well-rounded composition course needs to include a variety of modes of writing. Angela, Brad, and their students could benefit from listening to each other and carefully evaluating the writing students generate in response to each type of assignment.

A note of caution when inviting a student teacher of the opposite sex into your classroom: Students' interest in their teachers and capacity for fantasy can some- times lead them to imagine a romantic relationship behind the genial joking and obvious cooperation between professionals. This should not be a problem if age and marital status make this fantasy unlikely. Should this prevent a mentor– student teacher alliance when ages are closer? Certainly not, especially if both have similar ideas and approaches that mesh well. However, a mentor and a stu- dent teacher who are close in age may have to work more diligently at maintain- ing a professional demeanor in front of students to prevent any misconceptions.

Question 7: *Can I split my student teacher's time with one of my colleagues?*

Some universities allow the practice of splitting a student's teaching experience between two (or more) mentors. However, this is not a practice we recommend.

Although two colleagues may be alike in their teaching philosophies, they may be very different in their classroom practice, and these differences can cause problems for the student teacher. For example, the student teacher may be more comfortable with the teaching style of Mentor A and thus try to teach that way in Mentor B's class, causing confusion and possible resentment.

Another problem is time. In order for this practice to be successful, the two men- tors will need to meet daily to coordinate and plan strategies for working with the student teacher. In addition, each mentor will also need to meet with the student teacher for planning. A split assignment may place unreasonable time demands on both student teacher and mentors, especially if planning periods are not the same. In some cases, the student teacher may be given either too much or not enough responsibility, inadequately preparing her for the rigors of her own classroom.

Finally, the intensity of the student teacher–mentor relationship requires a level of commitment difficult to achieve when divided between two or more mentors. Progress and student teacher growth are more likely in a relationship of continuity with one mentor. The mentor may also find a one-on-one relationship richer and more rewarding.

Question 8: *What is my liability if my student teacher does something that is legally actionable?*

Mentors often worry about their legal liability in the event a student teacher does something that might be considered inappropriate or illegal. For example, what if the mentor steps out of the room and the student teacher physically reprimands a student by pushing him into his seat? Or what if the mentor suspects that the student teacher is too involved with a specific group of students and may be interacting with them outside of school? Or what if the student teacher is involved with drugs and it becomes obvious within the classroom? Who is liable—the student teacher, the mentor, the university, or the school district? These situations are extremely rare. The majority of student teachers are on their best behavior during student teaching because they are aware of the tremendous impact of this time on their lives and future careers. However, mentors may still be concerned.

In almost all cases, mentors are covered by insurance their districts or their professional organizations provide, so personal liability is unlikely to be an issue. However, let us quickly suggest responses to the above situations. It is acceptable for mentors to leave the room for a reasonable amount of time when a student teacher is in charge. Student teacher conduct outside school, even if it involves your students, is not your responsibility (though certainly you would wish to discourage inappropriate conduct if it comes to your attention). You would, of course, contact the university supervisor at once if you suspected the student teacher of substance abuse.

States differ on their interpretation of legal issues; however, basic legal tenets apply in most situations. If you are contemplating inviting a student teacher to come and work with you and are concerned about specific legal considerations, you should discuss these issues with the university supervisor or the placement official in your district or at the university.

Remember that the questions posed here are legitimate concerns but represent situations that rarely occur. In most cases, the student teaching situation presents an opportunity for professional growth for you and the student teacher.

Mentoring the Beginning Teacher

Question 1: *Will it be difficult to mentor someone who is considerably older or younger than I am?*

Although this question could also apply to the student teaching experience, the equality of two employees in the same district is more likely to create problems in the mentor-colleague relationship. Sometimes younger professionals feel that an older teacher will be very traditional and not up-to-date. Sometimes older professionals feel that younger teachers have not had enough professional experience to give credibility to their opinions. In reality, of course, these are stereotypes. Neither is necessarily accurate in individual cases.

As a mentor, you would be wise to spend some time with the assigned colleague early in the school year, becoming acquainted with teaching style and individual personality before forming a specific opinion or making a judgment. This time should also allow your new colleague to see you more clearly both personally and professionally.

However, no matter how professional the mentoring, there are times when age differences or issues become too great a barrier to a successful experience. If this occurs and both parties are uncomfortable, it may be time to consider requesting a reassignment. (We go into great detail on this subject in Chapter 3 of *Mentoring Across Boundaries: Helping Beginning Teachers Succeed in Challenging Situations* [Stenhouse].)

Question 2: *What if the person I've been assigned to mentor is really different from me as far as our professional background, methodological choices, and/or management styles?*

This may be one of the more difficult aspects of collegial mentoring, especially since what works for one person in terms of methodological choices may not work for another because of personality, instructional practice, or educational background. In addition, a mentor must remember that she may be teaching different courses and thus different levels of students than the colleague she is mentoring. It is easy to feel superior when a colleague reports disciplinary difficulties or poor student motivation; however, the difference may rest more with students than with teaching ability. Some classes would be challenges for anyone, and too often it is the newest and least experienced member of the department who is given these preparations.

As a mentor, then, it is important not to rely on your sense of the teacher you are now, but to remember what it was like to be the new colleague in the department who had no established reputation within the building. You must also remember that you are not the same teacher now that you were five or ten years ago, and that the colleague with whom you are working will change, adapt, and improve. Although differences in style sometimes make us uncomfortable, we can learn a great deal from a colleague who takes a different approach to instructional practice. Often, we would not consider certain opportunities if they were not suggested by what we saw or heard in our colleagues' classrooms, and this benefits all of us. Learning flows in both directions.

Question 3: *How much evaluation will I be expected to do? Will it be my responsibility to remediate this person?*

The mentoring program in your district may have certain expectations that you must fulfill, but most research suggests that evaluation should be separated from mentoring (Levine 1992). Ideally, then, your role should be that of supporter, not evaluator. It is unrealistic to expect a new colleague to be honest with you if she knows you must ultimately judge her performance. In most situations, the principal or a member of a formal mentoring team evaluates new teachers; this is preferable. Mentors more commonly find themselves being asked to provide thoughtful suggestions after peer classroom observations than to act in the role of gatekeeper.

Mentors are in a better position to suggest genuinely helpful remedial activities if they do not have an evaluative function. However, "evaluation" may take a variety of forms in any school. If you hope to be of real service to your new colleague, you must establish a relationship that merits trust. It will be critically important for you not only to avoid evaluative comments with your administrators (unless, of course, you are required to make them) but also to keep the concerns and the pedagogical performance of your colleague confidential in the lounge or lunchroom. The new teacher usually feels very anxious about the quality of his or her teaching performance and will certainly hesitate to confide in a mentor who repeats sensitive comments.

Your willingness to listen, encourage, console, and gently advocate for change may make the difference between a successful year and a discouraging year that drives a colleague from the field. Few opportunities can enable us to give a more valuable service to our colleagues or to our profession.

APPENDIX

Student Teacher Interview

The principal, English department chair, and potential mentor(s) may wish to interview student teachers prior to acceptance to determine whether they will fit in well with the goals and expectations of the school district. The interview could begin with one person providing information about the school district, such as student population, school district mission statement, department courses, class size, and other relevant information. Then the interviewers might ask some of the following questions to help determine whether the student teacher will be an effective match with the school district.

Possible Student Teacher Interview Questions

1. Tell us a little about yourself, your education, and your experiences.

2. Why did you choose to become a teacher?

3. Describe a successful experience you have had in working with students.

4. What is your philosophy of education? Tell us about some of your beliefs about teaching and learning.

5. How do you view your role as a student teacher?

6. What do you view as your mentor's role during your student teaching experience?

7. What is your philosophy of classroom management?

8. What is your philosophy of assessment? What types of methods would you like to use to determine how well students are learning?

9. Are there any special interests or activities with which you would like to become involved during your student teaching experience? For instance, are there any extracurricular activities/projects, faculty committees, or other areas you would like to observe or participate in?

10. What are your future goals after student teaching?

11. (Other questions specific to the school or area of teaching)

12. What questions would you like to ask us?

RESOURCES
FOR TEACHERS

✑ · Books · ✑

Action Research

Hendricks, Cher C. 2008. *Improving Schools Through Action Research: A Comprehensive Guide for Educators*. 2nd ed. Upper Saddle River, NJ: Allyn and Bacon.

Hubbard, Ruth Shagoury, and Brenda Miller Power. 2003. *The Art of Classroom Inquiry: A Handbook for Teacher-Researchers*. 2nd ed. Portsmouth, NH: Heinemann.

Mills, Geoffrey E. 2006. *Action Research: A Guide for the Teacher Researcher*. 3rd ed. Upper Saddle River, NJ: Prentice Hall.

Sagor, Richard. 2000. *Guiding School Improvement with Action Research*. Alexandria, VA: Association for Supervision and Curricular Development.

Beginning Teaching

Donoghue, Donna, Esther Collins, and Sally Wakefield. 2005. *A Guide for Beginning Elementary Teachers: From Getting Hired to Staying Inspired.* Portsmouth, NH: Teachers Ideas.

Wong, Harry, and Rosemary Wong. 2004. *The First Days of School: How to Be an Effective Teacher.* Mountain View, CA: Harry Wong.

Classroom Management

Canter, Lee, 2005. *Classroom Management for Academic Success.* Atlanta, GA: Solution Tree.

Canter, Lee, and Marlene Canter. 2001. *Assertive Discipline.* 3rd ed. Alexandria, VA: Association for Supervision and Curriculum Development.

Curwin, Richard, and Allen Mendler. 2001. *Discipline with Dignity.* Alexandria, VA: Association for Supervision and Curriculum Development.

DiGiulio, Robert. 2006. *Positive Classroom Management: A Step-By-Step Guide to Helping Students Succeed.* 3rd ed. Thousand Oaks, CA: Corwin.

Evertson, Carolyn, and Edmund T. Emmer. 2005. *Classroom Management for Elementary Teachers.* 8th ed. Upper Saddle River, NJ: Allyn and Bacon.

Faber, Adele, and Elaine Mazlish. 2005. *How to Talk so Kids Can Learn at Home and in School.* New York: Simon and Schuster.

Girard, Kathryn, and Susan J. Koch. 1996. *Conflict Resolution in the Schools: A Manual for Educators.* San Francisco: Jossey-Bass.

Kohn, Alfie. 2001. *Punished by Rewards: The Trouble with Gold Stars, Incentive Plans, A's, Praise, and Other Bribes.* 2nd ed. Boston: Houghton Mifflin.

Nelson, Jane. 2006. *Positive Discipline.* Rev. ed. New York: Ballantine Books.

Curriculum Development

Jacobs, Heidi Hayes. 2004. *Getting Results with Curriculum Mapping.* Alexandria, VA: Association for Supervision & Curriculum Development.

Posner, George J., and Alan N. Rudnitsky. 2005. *Course Design: A Guide to Curriculum Development for Teachers.* 7th ed. Upper Saddle River, NJ: Allyn and Bacon.

Udelhofen, Susan K. 2005. *Keys to Curriculum Mapping: Strategies and Tools to Make It Work.* Thousand Oaks, CA: Corwin.

Wiles, Jon W., and Joseph Bondi. 2006. *Curriculum Development: A Guide to Practice.* 7th ed. Upper Saddle River, NJ: Prentice Hall.

English Language Learners

Au, Kathryn. 2005. *Multicultural Issues and Literacy Achievement.* Florence, KY: Lawrence Erlbaum.

Harmer, Jeremy. 2007. *How to Teach English.* New York: Pearson Longman.

Lesson Planning

Hunter, Madeline C. 1994. *Mastery Teaching: Instructional Effectiveness in Elementary and Secondary Schools, Colleges, and Universities.* Thousand Oaks, CA: Corwin.

Serdyukov, Peter, and Mark Ryan. 2007. *Writing Effective Lesson Plans: The 5-Star Approach.* Upper Saddle River, NJ: Allyn and Bacon.

Woodward, Tessa. 2001. *Planning Lessons and Courses: Designing Sequences of Work for the Language Classroom.* New York: Cambridge University Press.

Mentoring

Boreen, Jean, and Donna Niday with Mary Johnson. 2003. *Mentoring Across Boundaries: Helping Beginning Teachers Succeed in Challenging Situations.* Portland, ME: Stenhouse.

Brock, Barbara Louise, and Marilyn L. Grady. 2007. *From First-Year to First-Rate: Principals Guiding Beginning Teachers*. 3rd ed. Thousand Oaks, CA: Corwin.

Dunne, Kathy, and Susan Villani. 2007. *Mentoring New Teachers Through Collaborative Coaching: Linking Teacher and Student Learning*. San Francisco: WestEd.

Hicks, Cathy D., Neal A. Glasgow, and Sarah J. McNary. 2004. *What Successful Mentors Do: 81 Research-Based Strategies for New Teacher Induction, Training, and Support*. Thousand Oaks, CA: Corwin.

Jonson, Kathleen Feeney. 2008. *Being an Effective Mentor: How to Help Beginning Teachers Succeed*. 2nd ed. Thousand Oaks, CA: Corwin.

Scherer, Marge. 1999. *A Better Beginning: Supporting and Mentoring New Teachers*. Alexandria, VA: Association for Supervision and Curriculum Development.

Professional Development

Udelhofen, Susan K., and Kathy Larson. 2003. *The Mentoring Year: A Step-by-Step Program for Professional Development*. Thousand Oaks, CA: Corwin.

Professional Development Schools

Byrd, David M., and D. John McIntyre, eds. 1999. *Research on Professional Development Schools: Teacher Education Yearbook VII*. Thousand Oaks, CA: Corwin.

Darling-Hammond, Linda, ed. 2005. *Professional Development Schools: Schools for Developing a Profession*. 2nd ed. New York: Teachers College.

Teitel, Lee. 2003. *The Professional Development Schools Handbook: Starting, Sustaining, and Assisting Partnerships That Improve Student Learning*. Thousand Oaks, CA: Corwin.

Tunks, Jeanne. 2007. *A Framework for Research on Professional Development Schools*. Lanham, MD: University Press of America.

Reflection

Adams-Bullock, Ann, and Parmalee P. Hawk. 2004. *Developing a Teaching Portfolio: A Guide to Preservice and Practicing Teachers*. 2nd ed. Upper Saddle River, NJ: Prentice Hall.

Foster, Bill R., Michael L. Walker, and Kim Hyunsook. 2006. *A Beginning Teaching Portfolio Handbook: Documenting and Reflecting on Your Professional Growth and Abilities*. Upper Saddle River, NJ: Prentice Hall.

McEntee, Grace Hall. 2003. *At the Heart of Teaching: A Guide to Reflective Practice*. New York: Teachers College.

Parsons, Rick, and Kimberlee Brown. 2001. *Teacher as Reflective Practitioner and Action Researcher*. Belmont, CA: Wadsworth.

Schön, Donald A. 1990. *Educating the Reflective Practitioner: Toward a New Design for Teaching and Learning in the Professions*. San Francisco: Jossey-Bass.

———. 1991. *The Reflective Turn: Case Studies in and on Educational Practice*. New York: Teachers College.

———. 1995. *The Reflective Practitioner: How Professionals Think in Action*. San Francisco: Jossey-Bass.

York-Barr, Jennifer, William A. Sommers, Gail S. Ghere, and Joanne K. Montie. 2005. *Reflective Practice to Improve Schools: An Action Guide for Educators*. Thousand Oaks, CA: Corwin.

Student Teaching

Graham, Peg, Sally Hudson-Ross, Chandra Adkins, Patti McWhorter, and Jennifer McDuffie Stewart, eds. 1999. *Teacher Mentor: A Dialogue for Collaborative Learning*. New York: Teachers College.

Podsen, India J., and Vicki M. Denmark. 2006. *Coaching and Mentoring First-Year and Student Teachers*. 2nd ed. Larchmont, NY: Eye on Education.

Schwebel, Sara L., David C. Schwebel, Bernice L. Schwebel, and Carol R. Schwebel. 2001. *The Student Teacher's Handbook*. 4th ed. Philadelphia: Lawrence Erlbaum.

✐ · Websites · ✐

Action Research

http://www.library.jhu.edu/researchhelp/education/actionresearch.html

http://gse.gmu.edu/research/tr

Beginning Teaching

http://www.geocities.com/Athens/Delphi/7862

Classroom Management

http://www.teachers.net/mentors/classroom_management

http://www.nea.org/neatoday

http://www.essdack.org/tips

http://www.classroommanagement.com

Curriculum Development

http://intercom.noeca.esu.k12.oh.us/downloads/npsp03.pdf

http://intercom.noeca.esu.k12.oh.us/downloads/CurriculumMappingProf.pdf

http://www.curriculummapping101.com/Curriculum_Mapping.html

Lesson Planning

The following sites include links to additional sites.

http://www.lessonstop.org

http://www.joplin.k12.mo.us

http://www.mv.com/org

http://www.teachweb.net

http://www.teacherspal.com

http://www.aces.k12.ct.us

http://www.teachers.net

http://www.4forefront.com

http://www.standardsplus.org

http://www.eChalk.com

http://teacherease.com

Mentoring

http://www.mentors.net/index.html

http://www.nsdc.org

http://nationalserviceresources.org/learns/mentoring-training

http://www.educ.msu.edu/alumni/newed/ne66c3~5.htm

http://www.teachermagazine.org/tm/index.html

http://www.edweek.org/ew/index.html

http://www.cec.sped.org/ericec/faqs.htm

Professional Development

http://www.ipfw.edu/dcs/workshops/default.shtml

http://doe.in.gov/asap/prodev.html

Professional Development Schools

http://www.education.qld.gov.au

Professional Organizations

The following Web addresses provide electronic mailing lists and chat rooms that teachers from a variety of disciplines may find useful. These lists are by no means exhaustive, but they may provide a starting point for any number of professional conversations.

Arts Education

National Art Education Association (NAEA)

http://www.naea-reston.org

Bilingual Education

California Association for Bilingual Education (CABE)
http://www.bilingualeducation.org

National Association for Bilingual Education (NABE)
http://www.nabe.org

Educational Technology

The Education Coalition—Distributed Learning Systems and Services
http://www.tecweb.org/index.html

International Technology Education Association
http://www.iteaconnect.org

English Education

The National Council of Teachers of English
http://www.ncte.org

The International Reading Association
http://www.reading.org

The Great Books Foundation
http://www.greatbooks.org

National Institute for Literacy
http://www.nifl.gov

History/Social Studies Education

National Council for the Social Studies
http://www.socialstudies.org

The Organization of History Teachers
http://www.historians.org

The National Council of Economic Education
http://www.ncee.net

Mathematics

Association of Teachers of Mathematics
http://www.atm.org.uk

National Council of Teachers of Mathematics
http://www.nctm.org

National Council of Supervisors of Mathematics
http://www.ncsmonline.org/OtherResources/listserv.html

Modern Languages

American Association of Teachers of French
http://frenchteachers.org

American Association of Teachers of German
http://www.aatg.org

American Association of Teachers of Spanish & Portuguese
http://www.aatsp.org

American Council on the Teaching of Foreign Languages
http://www.actfl.org

Computer Assisted Language Instruction Consortium
http://calico.org

National Network for Early Language Learning (NNELL)
http://www.nnell.org

Music Education

The National Association for Music Education
http://www.menc.org/

The Kennedy Center Arts Edge
http://artsedge.kennedy-center.org

Physical Education

National High School Coaches Association
http://www.nhsca.com

National High School Athletic Coaches Association
http://www.hscoaches.org

Science Education

National Association of Biology Teachers
http://www.nabt.org

National Center for Improving Student Learning and Achievement in Mathematics and Science
http://www.wcer.wisc.edu/NCISLA/index.html

National Science Teachers Association
http://www.nsta.org

American Association of Physics Teachers
http://www.aapt.org

Talented and Gifted Education

Center for Gifted Education
http://www.cfge.wm.edu

Professional Training for Teachers of the Gifted and Talented
http://www5.kidsource.com

California Association for the Gifted
http://www.cagifted.org

Council for Exceptional Children
http://www.cec.sped.org

National Association for Gifted Children
http://www.nagc.org

REFERENCES

Atwell, Nancie. 1998. *In the Middle: New Understandings About Writing, Reading, and Learning*. 2nd ed. Portsmouth, NH: Heinemann/Boynton-Cook.

Bey, Theresa M., and C. Thomas Holmes, eds. 1992. *Mentoring: Contemporary Principles and Issues*. Reston, VA: Association of Teacher Educators.

Bird, Lois Bridges. 1997. *Writing as a Way of Knowing*. York, ME: Stenhouse.

Brighton, Catherine. 1999. "Keeping Good Teachers: Lessons from Novices." In Marge Scherer, ed., *A Better Beginning: Supporting and Mentoring New Teachers*, pp. 197–201. Alexandria, VA: Association for Supervision and Curriculum Development.

Brock, Barbara L., and Marilyn L. Grady. 1997. *From First-Year to First-Rate: Principals Guiding Beginning Teachers*. Thousand Oaks, CA: Corwin Press.

Brownlow, Paul C., ed. 1995. *Dear Teacher: At 101 Words of Encouragement.* Fort Worth, TX: Brownlow.

Burke, Jim. 2007. *The English Teacher's Companion: A Complete Guide to Classroom, Curriculum, and the Profession.* 2nd ed. Portsmouth, NH: Boynton/Cook.

Carnegie Forum on Education and the Economy: Task Force on Teaching as a Profession. 1986. *A Nation Prepared: Teachers for the 21st Century*. New York: Carnegie Corporation.

Carroll, Thomas G. 2005. "Induction of Teachers into 21st Century Learning Communities: Creating the Next Generation of Educational Practice." *The New Educator* 1 (10): 199–204.

Christenbury, Leila. 2006. *Making the Journey: Being and Becoming a Teacher of English Language Arts*. 3rd ed. Portsmouth, NH: Boynton/Cook.

Costa, Arthur L., and Robert J. Garmston. 2002. *Cognitive Coaching: A Foundation for Renaissance Schools*. 2nd ed. Norwood, MA: Christopher-Gordon Publishers.

Cummins, Jim. 2003. "Basic Interpersonal Communicative Skills and Cognitive Academic Language Proficiency." http://www.iteachilearn.com/cummins/bicscalp.html.

Daniels, Harvey. 2001. *Literature Circles: Voice and Choice in Book Clubs and Reading Groups*. 2nd ed. York, ME: Stenhouse.

Danin, Rob, and Margaret A. Bacon. 1999. "What Teachers Like (and Don't Like) About Mandated Induction Program." In Marge Scherer, ed., *A Better Beginning: Supporting and Mentoring New Teachers*, pp. 202–209. Alexandria, VA: Association for Supervision and Curriculum Development.

Darling-Hammond, Linda, ed. 2005. *Professional Development Schools: Schools for Developing a Profession*. New York: Teachers College Press.

Dewey, John. 1910. *How We Think*. Boston: D. C. Heath.

Dillon, Sam. 2007. "Schools Scramble for Teachers Because of Spreading Turnover." *New York Times*, August 27.

Furlong, John, and Trisha Maynard. 1995. *Mentoring Student Teachers: The Growth of Professional Knowledge*. New York: Routledge.

Gardner, Howard. 2006. *Multiple Intelligences: New Horizons*. New York: Perseus.

Gonzales, Frank, and Alicia Sosa. 1993. "How Do We Keep Teachers in Our Classrooms? The TNT Response." *IDRA Newsletter* 1:6–9.

Goodlad, John I. 1984. *A Place Called School: Prospects for the Future*. New York: McGraw-Hill.

Gottesman, Barbara. 2000. *Peer Coaching for Educators*. Lanham, MD: Scarecrow Press.

Graham, Margaret. 1993. "Curious Positions: Exploring Tensions and Reciprocal Influences in Student Teachers' Relationships with Their Cooperating Teachers." Ph.D. diss., University of Iowa.

Halford, Joan Montgomery. 1998. "Easing the Way for New Teachers." *Educational Leadership* 55:33–36.

Hall, J. 2005. "Promoting Quality Programs Through State-School Relationships." In Hal Portner, ed., *Teacher Mentoring and Induction: The State of the Art and Beyond*, pp. 213–223. Thousand Oaks, CA: Corwin Press.

Holmes Group. 1986. *Tomorrow's Teachers: A Report of the Holmes Group*. East Lansing, MI: Holmes Corporation.

Hubbard, Ruth Shagoury, and Brenda Miller Power. 2003. *The Art of Classroom Inquiry: A Handbook for Teacher-Researchers*. Portsmouth, NH: Heinemann.

Huling, Leslie. 2001. "Teaching Mentoring as Professional Development." Washington DC: ERIC Clearinghouse on Teaching and Teacher Education. http://permanent.access.gpo.gov/websites/eric.ed.gov/ERIC_Digests.

Huling-Austin, Leslie. 1990. "Teacher Induction Programs and Internships." In W. Robert Houston, ed., *Handbook of Research on Teacher Education*, pp. 535–548. New York: Macmillan.

Ishler, Peggy. 1998. "Why Kathie and Others Quit Teaching." *Des Moines (IA) Register* (Des Moines, Iowa), January 24.

John-Steiner, Vera. 1997. *Notebooks of the Mind: Explorations of Thinking*. New York: Oxford University Press.

Karp, Hank, Connie Fuller, and Danilo Sirias. 2002. *Bridging the Boomer-Xer Gap*. Palo Ato, CA: Davies-Black.

LeClaire, Barbara. 2006. Interview by Donna Niday. October 8.

Levine, Marsha, ed. 1992. *Professional Practice Schools: Linking Teacher Education and School Reform*. New York: Teachers College Press.

Liesveld, Rosanne, and Jo Ann Miller. 2005. *Teaching with Your Strengths*. New York: Gallup Press.

Lortie, Daniel. 1975. *Schoolteacher: A Sociological Study*. Chicago: University of Chicago Press.

Marshall, James D., Peter Smagorinsky, and Michael W. Smith. 1995. *The Language of Interpretation: Patterns of Discourse in Discussions of Literature*. Urbana, IL: National Council of Teachers of English.

Moir, Ellen. 1999. "The Stages of a Teacher's First Year." In Marge Scherer, ed., *A Better Beginning: Supporting and Mentoring New Teachers*, pp. 19–23. Alexandria, VA: Association for Supervision and Curriculum Development.

Moir, Ellen, Janet Gless, and Wendy Baron. 1999. "A Support Program with Heart: The Santa Cruz Project." In Marge Scherer, ed., *A Better Beginning: Supporting and Mentoring New Teachers*, pp. 106–115. Alexandria, VA: Association for Supervision and Curriculum Development.

National Center for Education Statistics. 1999. "Teacher Quality: A Report on the Preparation and Qualifications of Public School Teachers." U.S. Department of Education. January. NCES 1999080.

National Commission on Excellence in Education. 1983. *A Nation at Risk: The Imperative for Educational Reform*. Washington, DC: U.S. Government Printing Office.

National Commission on Teaching and America's Future. 2003. *No Dream Denied: A Pledge to America's Children*. Washington, DC: Department of Education.

———. 2005. *Induction into Learning Communities*. Washington, DC: Department of Education.

Niday, Donna. 1996. "Beginning Again: Mentoring the Novice Teacher." Ph.D. diss., University of Iowa.

North Central Regional Educational Laboratory (NCREL). 2003. "A Process for Curriculum Mapping." *Note and Reflections* 4 (Spring): 1–5.

Nunan, David. 1990. "Action Research in the Language Classroom." In J. Richards and David Nunan, eds., *Second Language Teacher Education*. London: Cambridge University Press.

Odell, Sandra J. 1990. "Support for New Teachers." In Theresa Bey and C. Thomas Holmes, eds., *Mentoring: Developing Successful New Teachers*, pp. 3–24. Reston, VA: Association of Teacher Educators.

———. 1992. "Teacher Mentoring and Teacher Retention." *Journal of Teacher Education* 43 (3): 200–204.

Perkins-Gough, Deborah. 2003/2004. "Creating a Timely Curriculum: A Conversation with Heidi Hayes Jacobs." *Educational Leadership* 61 (4): 12–17.

Perl, Sondra, and Nancy Wilson. 1986. *Through Teachers' Eyes: Portraits of Writing Teachers at Work*. Portsmouth, NH: Heinemann.

Rankin, Jane. 2003. "Viewpoint." *Curriculum Technology Quarterly* 12 (3): 1–3.

Sadker, David, and Myra Sadker. 1994. *Failing at Fairness: How Our Schools Cheat Girls*. New York: Simon and Schuster.

Sagor, Richard. 2000. *Guiding School Improvement with Action Research*. Alexandria, VA: Association for Supervision and Curriculum Development.

Schön, Donald A. 1983. *The Reflective Practitioner: How Professionals Think in Action*. San Francisco: Jossey-Bass.

———. 1987. *Educating the Reflective Practitioner: Toward a New Design for Teaching and Learning in the Professions*. San Francisco: Jossey-Bass.

———. 1991. *The Reflective Turn: Case Studies in and on Educational Practice*. New York: Teachers College Press.

Slick, Gloria Appelt, ed. 1995. *Making the Difference for Teachers: The Field Experience in Actual Practice*. Thousand Oaks, CA: Corwin Press.

Sullivan, Cheryl Granade. 2004. *How to Mentor in the Midst of Change.* 2nd ed. Alexandria, VA: Association for Supervision and Curriculum Development.

Summers, J. A. 1987. *Summative Evaluation Report: Project CREDIT.* Terre Haute: Indiana State University, School of Education.

Tannen, Deborah. 2007. *You Just Don't Understand: Women and Men in Conversation.* New York: Ballantine Books.

Teitel, Lee. 2003. *The Professional Development Schools Handbook: Starting, Sustaining, and Assisting Partnerships That Improve Student Learning.* Thousand Oaks, CA: Corwin.

Tremmel, Robert. 1993. "Zen and the Art of Reflective Practice in Teacher Education." *Harvard Educational Review* 63 (4): 434–458.

Trubowitz, Sidney, and Maureen Picard Robins. 2003. *The Good Teacher Mentor: Setting the Standard for Support and Success.* New York: Teachers College Press.

Westerman, Delores. 1991. "Expert and Novice Teacher Decision Making." *Journal of Teacher Education* 42 (4): 292–305.

Zemelman, Steven, Harvey Daniels, and Arthur Hyde. 1998. *Best Practice: New Standards for Teaching and Learning in America's Schools.* 2nd ed. Portsmouth, NH: Heinemann.